Collins

need to know?

Tracing your family history

Anthony Adolph

Collins

First published in 2007 by Collins
an imprint of
HarperCollins Publishers
77–85 Fulham Palace Road
London W6 8JB

www.collins.co.uk

Collins is a registered trademark of
HarperCollins Publishers Limited

11 10 09 08 07
6 5 4 3 2 1

A catalogue record for this book is available from
the British Library

Designed and produced by Basement Press
Editor: Nicola Chalton
Designer: Pascal Thivillon
Series design: Mark Thomson

ISBN-13: 978-0-00-723545-2
ISBN-10: 0-00-723545-3

Colour reproduction by Printing Express Ltd, Hong Kong
Printed and bound by Printing Express Ltd, Hong Kong

To my mother, for having been unfailingly supportive

Contents

Family trees and the internet

New eras require new books. The internet has changed the way we trace family history, creating the need for a book that explains how to trace ancestry using the internet as a primary tool. This new approach to genealogy in the 21st century is the focus of this guide.

The importance of the internet

Genealogy's current popularity owes much to the way the internet has made information about ancestors accessible to everyone. The web has not only brought us this information but – and actually more importantly – it has indexed it. Instead of spending hours, days or weeks searching through documents to locate our ancestors, we can often find the people we want in seconds.

So 'easy' has the internet made searching for ancestors that you'd be foolish to try tracing your ancestors any other way. If you have no internet-enabled computer, you can get access to one at local libraries, record offices, internet cafés – or the homes of sympathetic friends or relatives. The internet has its pitfalls, of course, but these are minimal compared to the way it has made light of tasks that used to be terribly difficult.

While this 'need to know' book is written partly as a summary of my comprehensive guide to family history, *Tracing Your Family History*, I have also tried to make it the first practical guide to the subject that tackles the stages of tracing ancestry in the order that most people embarking on the adventure today actually encounter them.

Genealogy and family history

Tracing ancestry goes by two terms – genealogy, and family history. Genealogy (from the Greek *genea*, meaning 'race' or 'generation', and *logos* meaning 'knowledge') is the science of tracing ancestry by drawing together different sources of information to connect people of different generations. The result is also called 'a genealogy' and can be recorded in a narrative form (i.e. 'Edward was the son of Thomas, who in turn...') or using diagrams.

Genealogy is as old as human civilization. Records were always kept for a purpose. This might be to know who belonged to a tribe, a social group – such as the royal kin from whom new kings were chosen – or to determine rights to land and, more recently, to a title or coat of arms. The very earliest non-royal genealogy I have encountered dates from the oldest known human civilization. It is carved on an obelisk erected about 4,262 years ago by the Sumerian king Manishtushu, in what is now Iraq. It records his purchase of land from several perfectly ordinary farming families. Because the land was owned in shares by descendants of the original landowner, the king had to buy it from a number of interrelated people. Thanks to this, we have a genealogy of the descendants of several ancient Sumerians, particularly one Push-rab, 'ensi [lord] of Ki.utu', who lived about 4,300 years ago.

Even today, genealogies are relevant to modern life: we all, after all, hope to inherit our parents' worldly goods, and the ramifications of pedigree can go further. People who can produce a pedigree connecting them to Huguenot blood, for example, can, under certain circumstances, claim free

Historical trees

Possibly the earliest were the *stemma* painted in the atriums of Roman patricians' villas, showing their ancestors and usually their claimed descent from a Classical god. Such charts looked like trees, and were much later termed 'family trees'. The term 'pedigree' comes from the French *pied de grue*, meaning 'crane's foot', because in the Middle Ages family trees often took the form of names written in circles connected by radiating lines that (they thought) resembled the footprints left by cranes on the muddy shores of rivers. Family trees are usually now of the 'drop line' variety, which places the earliest known ancestor at the top of the page, with successive generations arranged below and connected together by straight right-angled lines.

treatment at the Huguenot hospital of La Providence in Rochester, Kent. I spoke recently to a girl whose ancestry was part British and part Philippine, including both native Philippinos and Spanish colonialists. In London, she applied for a government arts grant available to people from racial minorities and, in order to qualify, she had to produce a pedigree proving that she did indeed have some native Philippine (and thus non-European) blood in her veins.

True family history dates back no further than the early 20th century, particularly to Aleyn Lyell Reade's work on the family history of Dr Johnson, in which he tried to find out as much as he could about the economic and religious circumstances of the Johnson family to explain through its social history how it developed the way it did, and to tell the stories of members of the family in as much detail as possible. The finished results of family history research – if they can ever truly said to be 'finished', as there is always more to find out – are usually presented in a written format, accompanied by pictures of ancestors and of places where they lived and worked, either published in manuscript form or as family web pages on the internet.

Why we trace our ancestry

Tracing ancestry is very popular now because of the internet, but computers did not create the interest in the first place. Throughout the mid-late 20th century, as leisure time and prosperity increased in Britain, ever increasing numbers of people were starting to do it. The advent of personal computers has greatly facilitated this, but in doing so it has simply encouraged an existing trend. What I believe underlies our fascination with ancestry is not, ultimately, titles, financial benefits, coats of arms or even connections between living people. At the very core of our fascination with ancestry is the ability to point to a piece of land on a map – or better still visit it in person – and say, just as the descendants of the Sumerian Push-rab did in 2,255 BC 'my ancestors lived there!'

This book is what you need to know to be able to do the same.

Connections between the past and present: my great-great-aunt Louisa Havers (1832–1937) in 1917, with her young cousin Philip Coverdale who, as an old man, took me under his wing and taught me how to trace family trees.

1 Find your family

You can trace your family history entirely alone, but it's better with the help of relatives and friends. Existing family connections are very useful for finding out about your close relations, and the internet is an excellent way to make new contacts and spread your research further. The knowledge you gain can be recorded in a family tree, which is a good way to see your progress at a glance.

Making contact

The internet has made finding new contacts easier than ever before. There's a vast network of family historians out there, many of whom will be happy to help and may even be researching the same names as you. Also, remember to ask your close relatives: they, too, can be a mine of vital information.

must know
When to pay
Some of the websites cited here are free, but many ask for a small fee in return for their information. Equally, much original data both on and off the internet costs money (for example, General Registration certificates). I have not suggested any sites that are not worth the money they charge.

Searching on the internet

When I was first shown how the internet worked I was presented with a search engine and told 'you can look up anything you want'. My mind went completely blank for a moment, and then I thought I'd key in my surname and see what appeared. Right from the start, the internet has been ideally suited to looking up names, and from this has grown an amazing network of connections between genealogists that spans the globe. There now exists a truly 'world wide web' of family ties that genealogists could only dream about before.

Search engines such as www.google.co.uk and www.altavista.co.uk are ideal places to key in the surnames of your parents and grandparents, and see what comes up. Within minutes, you'll start to see whereabouts the surnames occur, whether anyone with these names was famous and if anyone on the internet has included your surnames in their own web pages. There are a huge number of family history websites and you can hone your searches by typing the surname plus key phrases such as 'genealogy' or 'family tree'.

These searches will give you an idea of what's out there for you. You may immediately find people who are definitely your kith and kin, in which case you can of course contact them. More likely, you'll find sites containing people who could be related to you, but you won't be sure. Make a note of these, or drop them an email simply to make contact. They may already know how your family fits into the bigger picture.

What to research

As your family tree grows, you'll discover the names of your great-grandparents, great-great-grandparents and so on. Unless you find cousins intermarrying, or an illegitimacy where the father's identity isn't known, the number of ancestral names will double with each generation that you trace back. Don't try tracing all these lines at once – you'll probably go mad in the attempt. Do a few at a time. But there are no rules as to which you should trace first – just chose the one, or several, that you find most intriguing and follow them.

Contact websites

There are some key places on the internet where you can make your interests known and have a high chance of finding people who are researching the same surname. In my experience (though as with most things on the internet, there are many more to chose from), the most useful are:

http://genforum.genealogy.com
www.curiousfox.com
www.list.jaunay.com
http://lists.rootsweb.com
http://boards.ancestry.com

These give different opportunities to register your interest on message boards dedicated to specific surnames and places (Rootsweb also includes message boards on other topics such as ancestral occupations). You may find people researching the same families as you, who can help you – or perhaps you'll be able to help them.

More sophisticated yet are sites in which you can enter the information you already know about your family tree – even if it's just your parents' names – so that you can be found by anyone else tracing the same families. The most prominent contact sites include:

> www.genesreunited.com
> www.ancestry.myfamily.com/trees/awt
> http://worldconnect.genealogy.rootsweb.com

I am the resident genealogist for Genes Reunited and have used it successfully time and again for private and media research. Besides adding your family details, you can use the site's search facility to look up any names you want and see if anyone out there is researching them. You may find instant matches (the site will automatically alert you if anyone else enters

The Genes Reunited website home page: www.genesreunited.com

names that are already in your tree), or you may simply find people who are researching the same surnames in the same areas, with whom you can co-operate. The site's database is now so large that in most cases I will find someone in the latter category, and increasingly it is producing exact matches for the names I enter. When I researched the actor Sir David Jason's family recently (see p. 65) I found twelve people on Genes Reunited who were descended from the same people as him – I even discovered that one of them was also a cousin of a cousin of mine!

What to ask

Of course, the internet's not the only tool at your disposal. You can and indeed should ask for the help of everyone in your immediate family. Your parents and any older relatives can tell you their own memories, which you can record in writing, by audio or video tape, or on digital media – most digital cameras now have a facility for 'filming' people. If you 'interview' people by email, then you will have a ready-made 'archive' of messages that you should keep safely.

watch out!
Don't neglect to make contact with younger relatives, who may remember things told them by deceased older ones.

For each relative in turn, the key points to ask are:
- The full name and nicknames
- When and where born
- Where educated
- Occupation(s)
- When and where married (if applicable)
- When and where died and buried
- Religion/religious denomination
- Interesting stories

Finally, ask the relative you're interviewing for contact details for any other relatives that they have in common with you. By doing this, you can 'network' your way outwards to ever more distant cousins, all of whom will hopefully be able to add to your knowledge of your family tree.

My great-great-grandparents, Albert Joseph Adolph and his wife Emily Lydia, née Watson. When I started my research, they were as far back as my grandfather's memory stretched.

Useful tip

Besides asking your family and registering with internet contact sites, you can track down living relatives using databases of telephone directories (and the telephone directory enquiries services) and electoral registers (see p. 93). The most useful website is www.192.com, which includes telephone directories and electoral registers going back several years, and other sources such as the register of all British company directors. The site is also adding new information specifically to help family historians, such as General Registration and census data. Another useful site is www.infobel.com, which covers many foreign countries in addition to the UK.

How to ask

How you ask is important too. Be courteous – 'Please could you tell me what was…' gets a better reception than 'What was…' – and always thank people who help you. Make your questions as clear as you can and include all relevant information.

Wrong: I can't find my gr gr granddad in the 1891 census was he in the army?
Right: I cannot find my great-great-grandfather Thomas Hobson, born in Ludlow, Shropshire, in 1865, in the 1891 census. I think this may be because he had joined the army. Do you know how I can find records that might prove or disprove this, please?

Also, stick to the point and don't confuse your reader with extraneous verbiage – and for goodness' sake, do your recipient the courtesy of obeying the rules of grammar and punctuation. Here is the previous example re-written in a style that's becoming all too familiar:

ive been tracing my family tree for five years now and have hit a complete brick wall I have been really successful tracing my mother's parsons ancestors right back to 1590 but that's another story anyway sorry to ramble on now, but the real problem is my gg grandad thomas hobson born ludlow in 1865 ludlows a really nice place in shrops that we visited last year when we won a competition for a free weekend stay at a b & b…

In the picture
It's worth asking people whether they have any pictures of your relatives or ancestors. Original pictures – paintings, miniatures, caricatures and photographs – are often treasured heirlooms, but now, with the advent of scanners, it's easy to make copies of them and send them to relatives all over the world, or place them on personal web pages.

You may think that I'm labouring this point, but unclear, rambling questions probably account for 50 per cent of all problems faced by modern family history researchers. I cannot overemphasize how much you should try to avoid this pitfall by spending a few extra minutes checking that your messages are clear and concise.

Old photographs can create a fantastic talking-point and draw out all sorts of unexpected family stories.

How much does it cost?

In this book I'm not going to recommend anything that's not inherently good value for money, but only you can decide when to start – and when to stop – spending money on your family history research. Be prepared to make at least a small expenditure on your research. It could save you money in the end by leading you straight to the right ancestors instead of on long, tortuous routes to the wrong ones. If money is limited, set a budget of how much you're prepared to spend each month. Bear in mind that the information costs vastly less online in terms both of pounds and time than it did only 15 years ago, when all searching involved lengthy journeys to spend long hours in the archives.

watch out!

Ultimately, you'll waste a lot of time, and probably money too, by trying to do all your family history research for nothing by not paying for any internet subscriptions or original documents.

How accurate is the information?

In research, there are two sorts of sources, primary and secondary. A primary record is one made at or near the time. This may be a document such as a census return (see p. 28), which you can see in its original state, or as a scanned image on the internet. It may, equally, be someone's personal knowledge of who their parents and grandparents were, written in a family Bible or typed as a page on the internet. Primary records might not be accurate, but generally you can work on the assumption that they are, unless proved otherwise.

Secondary sources are anything that is not primary. These include indexes and transcriptions (such as the data on www.familysearch.org) and family trees researched by other people (such as those on www.genesreunited.com). These may be stunningly accurate, but they may contain errors, or, in the worst cases, may just be made up.

Ultimately, unless it comes from a source you know you can trust (a family tree compiled by a very thorough genealogist who can back their work up with primary sources, for example), you will eventually want to check all data found in secondary sources against primary sources yourself. Of course, it's impractical to do this immediately, so in the interim just remember that if something you find in a primary source contradicts a secondary source, the latter's much more likely to be wrong. And if two secondary sources contradict each other, don't waste time trying to work out which is likelier to be true — go to the primary records at once!

must know
Accuracy
You won't go wrong if you remain aware that secondary information is there simply as a guide, and may or may not be accurate. To be sure of accuracy, go to primary sources.

Keeping records

One of the most important things to remember when collecting information about your family is to make a record of everything you find out. These records will form the basis of your family tree.

Writing it all down

Keep records of everyone you contact and what they have said. By the same token, keep careful notes of all records you see on- and off-line. A good way of arranging data is in narrative format, starting with the earliest ancestor you've traced at the top:

Alfred Williamson
Write everything you know about this ancestor here. Then list his children:
  1 **Eustace Williamson**, the next member of the direct line, so after his name type 'see below'.
  2 **Thomas Williamson**. If you've got anything to say about Thomas and his descendants, you can write it here.
  3 **Emma Williamson**
  4 **Frederick Williamson**. If you have absolutely loads of information on Fred and his descendants, you may want to open a separate 'chapter' for him and put him at the top of his own narrative document.
Eustace Williamson, son of Alfred.
You can now write what you know about him, and so on for all members of the direct line down from him.

You can also type up your family tree in any of the wide variety of software packages available. Choosing a 'package' to suit you is a matter of taste. Samples and sometimes full packages are often given away free by magazines such as *Your Family Tree*. An excellent table comparing their strengths and weaknesses is at www.My-history.co.uk. Many are based in 'Gedcom' format. The advantage of Gedcom is that once you've typed your data into one Gedcom-based package, you can transfer the information easily into any other. Genes Reunited is Gedcom-based, so you can either import existing files into it or export a family tree typed in the site to other packages.

The advantages of computer packages are great – they are easy to transfer, copy and update. Disadvantages are that they can sometimes reduce ancestors and their 'vital data' (birth, marriage and death dates, for example) to mere commodities and make you forget that you're dealing with real people. Also, some demand data such as a year of birth that you might not know, and force you – and I cringe as I write this – to 'estimate' one.

There are alternatives. You can draw a family tree by hand on a large sheet of paper, or type one using Microsoft Word or – better still – QuickCAD. The latter was designed for architects, but is very flexible and easy to adapt for family tree designing purposes.

Whether you keep records on paper stored in cardboard files or envelopes, or in files created on your computer – I suggest that you have one file per family surname. Don't forget to back up computer files and to cross-reference them with any original documents and photographs kept elsewhere.

1 Find your family

This is an example of how to set out information in a 'drop-line' family tree.

Frances
b. 24 May 1736
bpt. 25 May 1736
bur. 31 May 1736
Stowmarket, Suffolk

Mary
b. 9 June 1738
bpt. 26 June 1738
Stowmarket

Pedigree conventions

There are some sensible conventions and abbreviations, which you'll need to know both for compiling your own family tree and understanding other peoples'. These are as follows:

= Indicates a marriage, accompanied by 'm.' and the date and place

— Solid lines indicate definite connections

.... Dotted lines indicate probable but unproven ones

∿ Wiggly lines are for illegitimacy and 'x' for a union out of wedlock — important on old pedigrees but less relevant today

↯ Loops are used if two unconnected lines need to cross over

● Wives usually go on the right of husbands, though only if that doesn't interfere with the overall layout of the chart

● Conventionally, surnames are put after men's but not women's names, but again this is becoming a bit old-fashioned

b. born

bpt or c. baptised or christened (same thing)

bach. bachelor

bur. or sep. buried

coh. coheir(ess)

d. or ob./obit. died

d.s.p. or o.s.p. died without children

d.v.p. or o.v.p. died before father

ed. educated

fl. lived ('floreat')

inft infant

k.i.a. killed in action

lic. marriage licence

m. or = married

m. diss. by div. marriage dissolved by divorce

m.i.w. mentioned in the will of, followed by **f.** for father, **gf.** for grandfather and so on

MI monumental inscription

spin. spinster

temp. in the time of

unm. unmarried

wid. widow or widower (as appropriate)

w.wr./pr. will written/proved

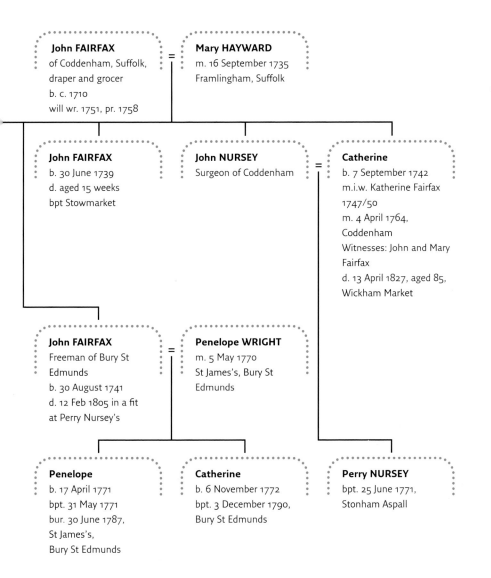

John FAIRFAX
of Coddenham, Suffolk,
draper and grocer
b. c. 1710
will wr. 1751, pr. 1758

=

Mary HAYWARD
m. 16 September 1735
Framlingham, Suffolk

John FAIRFAX
b. 30 June 1739
d. aged 15 weeks
bpt Stowmarket

John NURSEY
Surgeon of Coddenham

=

Catherine
b. 7 September 1742
m.i.w. Katherine Fairfax
1747/50
m. 4 April 1764,
Coddenham
Witnesses: John and Mary
Fairfax
d. 13 April 1827, aged 85,
Wickham Market

John FAIRFAX
Freeman of Bury St
Edmunds
b. 30 August 1741
d. 12 Feb 1805 in a fit
at Perry Nursey's

=

Penelope WRIGHT
m. 5 May 1770
St James's, Bury St
Edmunds

Penelope
b. 17 April 1771
bpt. 31 May 1771
bur. 30 June 1787,
St James's,
Bury St Edmunds

Catherine
b. 6 November 1772
bpt. 3 December 1790,
Bury St Edmunds

Perry NURSEY
bpt. 25 June 1771,
Stonham Aspall

Case history

J.K. Rowling's mystery great-grandfather

Tracing writer J.K. Rowling's family tree went well until I reached her maternal grandmother, known as Freda, who was born Louisa Caroline Watts Smith on 6 May 1916 at a private nursing home, 6, Fairmead Road, the illegitimate daughter of Mary Smith, a book-keeper.

That could have been the end of the line. Seeking the birth of a Mary Smith in General Registration without knowing her age would have been well-nigh impossible. Luckily, though, when I keyed Louisa's name into GenesReunited, I found her, entered by her daughter Marion Fox – J.K. Rowling's aunt. Marion told me that Freda grew up with foster parents, the Wattses, and was told when she was 18 that her father was a Doctor Campbell, who paid for her upkeep. When Freda was born, Mary gave her address as 42 Belleville Road, Clapham. A search of medical and post office directories for the years around 1916 revealed only one Dr Campbell in South London – Dugald Campbell, M.B., C.M., of 57 Josephine Avenue, Brixton, little more than two miles' omnibus ride away from Mary's address. Although one can never be 100 per cent certain in cases of illegitimacy, the facts fit Marion's family story remarkably well.

J.K. Rowling's mystery great-grandfather Dugald Campbell was from Lamlash, Argyll, and also served in Hawaii. The hospital he established at Waimea there honours his memory to this day. He was an extraordinary ancestor of J.K. Rowling's, one whom I could never have found without the family knowledge I obtained via Genes Reunited.

Expanding on the basics

When it comes to writing up the family history, you can decide what to say and how to say it. You can obtain ideas from the case studies in this book and the many published family histories and articles in family history journals and magazines.

It's a good idea to try to relate the events in the family to the world around them:

- Who was on the throne?
- What wars and plagues could have affected them?
- What were the places where they lived like at the time?
- What did their occupations entail?

This is a valuable exercise, which might actually help you find out more about your ancestors, or highlight inaccuracies or even mistakes in your family tree. It's also a good reminder that these were real, breathing people who existed in the world, not as pale shadows on old, dusty records. The more you can think of ways to convey the idea of your ancestors as human beings, the more fun – and success – you're likely to have tracing your family history.

want to know more?

- Many published family histories have been deposited at the Society of Genealogists (see pages 83 and 163). Their catalogue is a sort of super-bibliography of work done previously and can be searched online at www.sog.org.uk/sogcat /index.html.
- You can seek pictures of ancestors (usually, though by no means always, of the better-off sort) using the National Portrait Gallery's database of over 330,000 portraits and engravings, part of which is online at www.npg.org.uk/search.

2 Censuses

Census returns record where everybody in the
land was on census night, detailing their
names, ages, occupations, places of birth and
relationship to one another. They are effectively
snapshots taken of our ancestors in the past
and, especially because they record ages and
places of birth, they are a formidable
genealogical tool.

Censuses online

April 2006 marked a massive milestone in genealogy, for now all genealogically useful censuses are online. Wherever you are in the world, you can look your ancestors up in the censuses from 1901 back to 1841 and see images of the original enumerator's pages that recorded them.

must know

Where to begin

The most recent census currently available for public research is for 1901, the year Queen Victoria died. Most people's family knowledge, supplemented where possible by that of older relatives, will stretch back to 1901. If not, you can establish who your ancestors were that year using General Registration (see chapter 3). Then you can look them up in the 1901 census return.

Censuses available

Although censuses have been taken every ten years since 1801 (except 1941, because of the War), secrecy legislation means that they are only available for public searching from 1901 back. Those for 1911 will be released in 2012. With a handful of exceptions, censuses before 1841 do not include names, so are no use to us.

Censuses exist as paper books, compiled by enumerators who went door to door to collect the data. They have been available for public searching on microfilm for the past half century, with various indexes to parishes, streets and, in some cases, people, compiled mainly by volunteers in local family history societies. Despite their monumental efforts, most material was never indexed, and locating your ancestors in a census depended on finding their address from a directory or General Registration record, or simply slogging through the enumeration books for the place where you thought they lived. It was terribly hard work, and often didn't result in success.

In 1999, the 1881 census for England and Wales was fully transcribed and indexed by the Mormon Church (or Church of Jesus Christ of Latter-Day

Saints), whose innocuous mission is to identify everyone's ancestors and posthumously baptise them into the Mormon faith. The result was launched on the web at www.familysearch.org. The Government did the same for the 1901 census in 2002 (this site was bought by www.genesreunited.com in 2005). Since then, all the censuses, including their own transcriptions of the 1881 and 1901 returns, have appeared on www.ancestry.com. The last to appear was the 1841 census, released on 24 April 2006. Other companies offering some of the censuses online, at different costs, include www.1837online.com, www.britishorigins.com and www.192.com. Sections of census returns are freely available at http://freecen.rootsweb.com and via http://www.censusfinder.com.

Now all the censuses you'll need are online. This is the homepage of the 1901 census (www.census.pro.gov.uk).

Censuses outside England and Wales

• Records for the Channel Islands and the Isle of Man are largely separate from mainland ones and are housed in archives on the island concerned. The main addresses for seeking censuses, General Registration, wills, parish registers and so on are given in the address section at the end of this book.

• Scottish censuses (1901-1841) are indexed online at www.scotlandspeople.gov.uk

• Censuses for Ireland were mostly destroyed by IRA bombing and government space-saving efforts, except for 1901 and 1911, which are available at Ireland's two national archives in Dublin and Belfast. Pre-1901 survivals are listed in J.G. Ryan's *Irish Records – Sources for Family and Local History*, Ancestry (rev. edn, 1997). Applications for old-age pensions up to 1921 that included extracts of later-destroyed censuses are at www.pensear.org (and at the Irish National Archives, Public Record Office of Northern Ireland and Society of Genealogists in London).

A census enumerator collects a completed census form.

How to search censuses

Assuming you know the name of an ancestor who was alive in 1901, you can seek them in the 1901 census. Hopefully, they will appear in a household with their siblings and parents. Armed with the parents' names, you can then seek them in the 1891 census, and work back through the decades until you find them living with their own parents. If all goes smoothly, you can work back to the 1851 census (1841 is not so detailed or so useful), where you'll find your earlier ancestors stating their ages and places of birth in the early 1800s. If you are very lucky, you'll find them living with parents or even grandparents who were born in the mid-late 18th century. You can then expand and verify your family tree back to 1837 using General Registration records (see chapter 3), and then seek the origins of the earliest ancestors in parish registers (see chapter 4).

If the search back to 1851 doesn't go smoothly, don't worry – you can start the General Registration process earlier, and this should get you back on the right track.

Most sites invite you to key in the name of your ancestor. If it's a rare one, this is all you will need to make them appear on an index page that will lead you to the right entry. If it's a popular name, you can refine your search by adding additional information to your search criteria – this might be where you think they lived, or where or when (even roughly) they were born. With very common combinations of names even this will result in a long list of possibilities. You may be able to refine the search further if you have other co-ordinates on the family – the name of another sibling, perhaps, who will hopefully appear under the same reference as the first person. But if all else fails, then by checking each possibility in turn you will in almost all cases be able to find your ancestor.

Variant spellings

The greatest problem you are likely to face when using census returns is your ancestor not appearing under the exact name or age you expected. The original returns contain inaccuracies – ages given incorrectly and names spelled as the enumerator heard them. By the same token, the transcribers of the online indexes made numerous errors of their own when transcribing old handwriting. Therefore, seek your ancestor under any variant spelling you can imagine, such as Mumey instead of Murray (a real example from the 1861 census), Homes instead of Holmes and so on. Mumble the surname and see what people think you're saying (my best example is 'Coldbreath', which I mumbled to someone who thought I was saying Galbreith: it transpired that the former is indeed a recognized variation of the latter). Also, scribble the surname and its variants down in a variety of ways and see what other people think your scribbles say. I've just scribbled 'Cassidy' and it looks like 'Gamily' and that's how it may appear in a census index.

Of course, if you find someone under a radically different surname, you mustn't just accept it is your ancestor – you should seek further co-ordinates using records described later on in this book. But it will give you something to work on.

Birthplaces, of course, were where people thought they originated, and so can be wrong, or generalized.

watch out!

Before 1876, when it became compulsory for children under 13 to attend school, most people were illiterate so had no notion of spelling. When searching under a name, be sure to try different spellings.

Someone born in a village outside a town might say
they were born in the town. If the family moved
while the person was a baby, the person may
incorrectly say they were born in the place where
they grew up. Immigrants, especially Irish ones,
fearing repatriation (they had no need to fear) often
said they were born 'here!'

Details in the returns

Houses are separated by double dashes, and
individual households within the same buildings by
single ones. '-in-law' and 'step-' were often used
interchangeably. Adopted, foster or step-children
could simply be recorded as 'son' or 'daughter'. In
the 'marital condition' column, 'M' meant 'married',
'S' meant single and 'W' was for a widow or widower.
The 1891 and 1901 returns state if the person was an
employer or not, and if they were, how many people
worked for them. The last column records physical
and mental handicaps.

A page from the 1901 census.

Census of 1841

The 1841 census differs from its later peers by being much less detailed. Ages, except for children, were generally rounded down to the nearest five years, so, for example, someone aged anything from 30 to 34 would be recorded as 30. Relationships were not stated, so don't assume that a 30-year-old and a 3-year-old living together were parent and child – it could be uncle and nephew. Precise addresses were seldom given, so the households just appear as a list under the overall heading of the village or town. Places of birth are just given as 'yes' or 'no' to the question 'were you born in this county?' Despite this, the census of 1841 is very useful, especially for ancestors who did not survive until 1851.

A page from an 1841 census return.

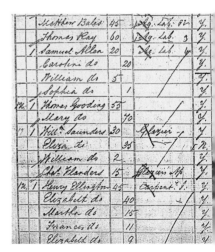

Case history

Ronnie Corbett's tragic family tale

Researching comedian Ronnie Corbett's family tree revealed a surprisingly sad story of depravation and death. Born in Edinburgh in 1930, the diminutive entertainer's ancestry went back smoothly to his grandfather, Walter Corbett, born at Thornybank, Edinburgh, in 1873. Walter's Scottish birth, marriage and death certificates all confirmed that his parents were William Corbett and Isobel Cuthbert, a couple who claimed to have been married, but who were in fact a common-law couple.

The 1871 census, accessible at www.scotlandspeople.gov.uk, shows the family two years before Walter's birth. William Corbett was a 39-year-old coal merchant born in St Cuthbert's, Edinburgh, and Isobel was 34, born in Perth. They had five children, from 11 years to 4 months, but despite this they shared their tenement, which had only two windowed rooms (Scottish censuses are more detailed than English ones in this respect), with William's sister Jessie, 22, a servant and her illegitimate 3-month-old baby William.

Of William and Isobel's sons, John does not appear alongside his new brother Walter in the 1881 census. The reason emerged from *The Scotsman*, 21 September 1874:

> About two o'clock on Saturday afternoon, a boy of ten years, named John Corbett, son of a coal dealer at Thorniebank, was drowned while bathing in the Union Canal near No. 3 bridge. The unfortunate lad, after saying he could show his companions the way to dive, jumped into the water beyond his depth, and being unable to swim, sank before assistance could be rendered.

It's a tragic tale, but a good example of how a few records can paint a vivid picture of an 'ordinary' family in the 1870s.

Searching manually

One of the advantages of censuses online is they are automatically indexed. However, if you can't find the ancestor you want in the online censuses, you can always turn back the clock and search for them using more traditional means. The Family Records Centre has them all on microfiche, with all the available finding aids and indexes. Your local Mormon Family History Centre (contact details are on www.familysearch.org) will obtain relevant microfiche films for you by post. Many can be bought in sections on CD-ROM from www.genealogysupplies.com.

The truth about censuses

Always bear in mind that you are not looking at a set of records made for family historians of the future. These are gritty records compiled to assess how many men could be called to arms, and how overpopulated these islands were becoming. They were made on Sunday nights, whatever the weather, by tired enumerators going from door to door. These are fantastically detailed records, but don't always expect text-book accuracy!

want to know more?
• The whereabouts of all census indexes is given in J. Gibson and E. Hampson's *Marriage and Census Indexes for Family Historians* (FFHS, 2000). Many are also listed at www.family historyonline.net.
• If no indexes exist, you can seek addresses where the family may have been living by using directories (see p.91) and General Registration records (see chapter 3) and look them up manually.

3 Births, marriages and deaths

Family knowledge and censuses give you an outline family tree, but it will lack firm dates and places of birth, marriage and death. The records compiled for General Registration are essential tools when it comes to filling in the details of your family tree. This is the next step once you've traced the outline and should be done *before* you try to trace back earlier than 1841.

General Registration

General Registration of births, marriages and deaths started on 1 July 1837 and continues to the present day. By seeking General Registration records for all your direct ancestors (great-grandparents, great-great-grandparents and so on) you can achieve a detailed and interesting family tree.

Seeking records

Seeking births and marriages is rather like tag-team wrestling, where one person does his job and then hands over to his partner, who then does their work and hands the fight back. Once you have someone's birth certificate, it will tell you who the parents were. You can then seek the marriage of this couple prior to the birth. Their marriage certificate will provide the couple's ages and name their fathers. Armed with this, you can then seek the births of all parties – you will know you've got the right certificates if the fathers' names match up.

Seeking deaths is harder, as you don't always know when people died – though family memories and the non-appearance of people in censuses is always a good clue. Sometimes it's just a question of

Marriage certificate of Patrick Henry Kilduff and Mary Ann Collingwood Paterson, 1879.

searching forwards and hoping (rather cruelly, I always think) that they didn't live too long. To cut a long search short it's sometimes easier to seek deaths through will indexes (see pages 66–73), church burial records (page 59) or gravestones (page 93). Except in Scotland, death records aren't that useful for tracing ancestry, but they complete the story of your ancestors' lives: they tell you how they died, which is important to know if you're worried about inherited medical conditions. They are also good for giving precise ages of people who died before 1851, and the name of the informant of the death, who will usually be a close relative.

General Registration online

You can order records from the Registrar General at www.gro.gov.uk or by dialling 0845 603 7788. Certificates currently cost £7 if you supply the correct reference from the General Registration indexes (see page 40), or if you think you know the date of the event (but not the reference) they charge £10 for up to a three-year search. As you are tracing your ancestry (and they're not) you should always try to provide the correct reference yourself.

watch out!

A surprising number of brides walked up the aisle pregnant, so when searching for a marriage certificate, unless you know the couple had older children, start from the date immediately before the birth.

must know

Death certificates
These are another means of making sure that you really have traced the right people. 'Always kill off your ancestors' is a time-honoured piece of genealogical advice.

Death certificate of Rev. Patrick Henry Kilduff, 1917.

watch out!

Don't attempt to search General Registration records without knowing how these records and their indexes work – it's far too easy to arrive at the wrong conclusions.

At the time of writing – and there are plans to expand coverage – the site www.familyrelatives.org provides a single index to the periods 1866–1920 and 1984–2002. The site www.BMDIndex.co.uk also indexes the records between 1984 and 2003. An almost complete index for 1837–1901 is at www.freebmd.org.uk. The main indexes were compiled from the local indexes of the superintendent registrars who originally recorded the events. Some of their records are also being computerized and you can find details of what is available at www.ukbmd.org.uk. Finally, many one-name societies and individuals interested in single surnames have produced exhaustive lists of General Registration references to that name, for which see *General Register Office One-Name Lists in the Library of the SoG* (SoG, 1997).

Failing these resources – and, as indexes of indexes, they will have their errors and omissions – you may need to search the General Registration indexes yourself. You can do this at www.genesreunited.com or www.1837online.com, in microfiche form at Mormon Family History Centres and some local archives, or at the Family Records Centre.

The homepage for www.familyrelatives.org

Using General Registration indexes

Births, marriage and deaths are registered by local registrars, who report to the superintendent registrars of each of the country's registration districts. The Institute of Heraldic and Genealogical Studies produces useful maps of the country showing the boundaries of the registration districts. The superintendent registrars in turn send copies of the records to the Registrar General, whose department compiles the General Registration indexes. Indexes were compiled for each quarter of the year (January–March, called the March quarter, April–June, called the June quarter, etc). These became annual indexes in 1984. Note that marriages are always indexed in the quarters in which they took place, but births can be registered up to six weeks later, so may appear in the next quarter, and death registration can similarly be held up by lengthy inquests or post mortems.

Bear in mind that while you may think you know where an event took place, you don't know for sure until you have the certificate. Thus, you can start by searching for an event in a specific registration district, but don't be wrong-footed if it isn't there – broaden your search to the surrounding districts instead.

Checking certificates

When you apply for a certificate, you can have a check made for a piece of information you know should be there. If you know the father's name from a marriage certificate, for example, this can be a good 'checking point'. Then if the certificate you've

The Family Records Centre in Myddleton Road, London EC1, home of the General Registration indexes. Note that in 2008 it is closing and its entire content is to be housed at the National Archives at Kew.

must know

Local gen
You can find the registration district covering any parish, and much more useful information besides, at www.visionofbritain. org.uk and www.genuki.org.uk.

Useful tip

Note the possibility for error in the process of compiling General Registration indexes. If what you want isn't in the index, especially in the case of marriages, try the original, local records instead.

ordered doesn't match up, you'll be refunded £4. This system is especially useful if (as so often happens) you find several possible entries in the indexes and are not sure which is right. However, make sure you're not too restrictive on your checking criteria. The father may be down as John Aloysius Smith on the marriage record, but might have been given as plain John Smith on the birth certificate, so it's best to put 'John plus or minus other names Smith' as your check. Similarly, if you use ages as a checking point, say 'aged 23 plus or minus a year', never just '23'.

What birth records tell you

The indexes give the name (with initials instead of middle names), registration district and, from September 1911, the mother's maiden name. Sometimes, parents registered a birth before having decided the baby's name, and these entries appear at the end of the list, with the surname as 'male' or 'female'.

Birth certificates record:

• **Date and place of birth**. If the exact time of birth is given, the child probably belonged to a set of twins. Look in the General Registration index for other children born in the same quarter and district who could be your ancestor's twin.

• **Child's name**. Children's names can be added to or altered on birth certificates for up to a year after registration, unless a baptism has occurred. The child will appear in the indexes under both the original name (or lack of it) and a changed or added one, so this is unlikely to cause you problems.

• **Name and occupation of father**. Be cautious of occupational status: there are many instances of bankers' clerks saying they were bankers, cottagers claiming to be farmers, and so on.

- **Name and maiden name of mother**. Former married names are usually given in the form (for example) 'Rose Smith late Jones formerly Evans'. This means that Rose was born Rose Evans, married Mr Jones, was widowed or divorced and later married Mr Smith.
- **Signature or mark and address of informant**. This was normally a parent. Signing with a mark usually indicated illiteracy, but of course the signatory may merely have injured their hand. Sometimes, registrars incorrectly assumed that poor people could not sign their own names and invited them to make their marks instead, and the signatories were simply too deferential to speak up.

What marriage records tell you

The indexes give names, registration district and a reference number. Search by choosing the least usual of the two surnames and, when you find a possible reference to one party, see if there is a corresponding reference for the other, with an identical registration district and reference number. The reference numbers relate to pages containing two marriage entries – something you will notice using www.freeBMD.org.uk. There are a few unlucky cases in which John Smith and Mary Brown do indeed appear on the same page but as the groom and bride respectively in two completely different weddings! In such cases, you will simply have to continue the search once your application for the certificate has been returned. From March 1912, the name of the other spouse appears next to the relevant index entries, avoiding this problem and making searches much more straightforward.

Marriage certificates record:

• **Date and place of the marriage**. The parish was usually the home parish of the bride.

• **Names of bride and groom**. A widow is recorded under her last married name, not her maiden name.

• **Marital condition: bachelor or spinster, widower or widow**. If divorced, the name of the previous spouse may be recorded.

• **Ages**. These can be inaccurate. In many cases the bride and groom will simply state either 'full age' or 'minor'. 'Minor' means under 21. Until 1929, provided they had parental consent, boys could marry at 14 and girls at 12, and after 1929 the minimum age was 16. Marriages between such young people were rare, but they did happen sometimes. 'Full age' means 21 or over, or under 21 but lying to avoid the need for parental consent. Sometimes, couples lied about their ages to lessen large age differences.

• **Occupations**. Until the mid-20th century, even if she worked 18-hour days at a coal mine or scrubbing other peoples' doorsteps, the bride's occupation was very seldom deemed worthy of recording.

• **Place of residence**. Generally, the bride's address is likely to have been her normal address, but grooms often took up temporary residence in the parish, usually for a minimum of four weeks, in order to be allowed to marry in the parish church.

• **Names and occupations of fathers**. Mothers' names were not recorded. Fathers' occupations sometimes included an element of exaggeration – boatswains becoming captains, for example. If fathers were said to be dead, they probably were, but if this is not stated it is by no means a guarantee they were still alive!

• **Whether the marriage was by banns or licence**. See page 58.

• **Signatures or marks of bride, groom and a minimum of two witnesses**.

• **Name of clergyman** who might sometimes be a relation.

An Adolph family wedding in Hove, 1915.

What death records tell you

The indexes give the name and the district where the death was registered. Only from March 1866, unfortunately, are ages given in the indexes. From March 1969 the date of birth appears.

Death certificates record:

• **Name**.

• **Date and place of death**. This will usually be the deceased's house. However, hospitals were generally recorded simply by their postal address too.

• **Cause of death**. As you work back into the past, you'll find these statements become less informative. Many old people died in the 19th century of 'decay of nature'. If a coroner's inquest took place, this will be stated and you can look for it in local newspapers (see p. 99) and using *Coroners' Records in England and Wales* (FFHS, 1997) by J. Gibson and C. Rogers.

• **Age**. From June 1969, the date of birth is given instead. Bear in mind that informants often got the age of the deceased slightly wrong.

• **Occupation**. Married women and widows were sometimes described as 'wife' or 'widow' of their husband. Young children were usually described in terms of who their fathers were.

• **Name, address and signature or mark of the informant**. The informant was often a child of the deceased, or another close relative, so this section is very useful if you are trying to track down the deceased's living descendants. However, especially after 1874, informants might also be the doctor in attendance.

must know

Unrecorded events
Some events went unrecorded. Only in 1875 did parents become legally obliged to register their children's births, and were fined for not doing so.

Broadening your search

If you can't find an event in the records, it may be because no one registered it, but it's more likely to be because it appears in a different year or registration district, or under a variant spelling. People might appear under slightly different forenames – Ellen instead of Helen or Jack instead of John or James, for example. Never be scared of broadening your search – the checking process described above will help keep you from making errors. If all else fails, parish registers (see p. 52), which are still being kept, provide a useful fallback.

Many illegitimate children ended up in the workhouse, and their births went unrecorded.

Records in Scotland and Ireland

Scottish General Registration started on 1 January 1855. The site www.scotlandspeople.gov.uk has indexes and downloadable copies of the certificates for births 1855–1905, marriages 1855–1930 and deaths 1855–1955; coverage is increasing and will eventually be complete. In the interim, you can search the remaining years, for a small fee, at the Registrar General of Scotland's searchroom in Edinburgh (or by hiring a searcher there), or via a computer link, Scottish Link, at the Family Records Centre, London.

The Scottish records for the year 1855 are extremely detailed, as you'll see if you're lucky enough to find a family event taking place that year. Birth indexes from 1929 give mother's maiden names, and the certificates from 1861 include the date of the parents' marriage. Marriage indexes list women under maiden and married names, and certificates include the fathers and mothers of the

Away from home

There are other General Registration records at www.1837online.com and the Family Records Centre covering events outside England and Wales, including:

• Consular records of births, marriages and deaths of British subjects kept by British consuls from 1 July 1849.

• Birth and death at sea from 1 July 1837. See *All At Sea* by Christopher and Michael Watts (SoG publications) for more details.

• First and Second World War armed forces deaths.

• Armed forces births, baptisms, marriages and deaths (except the two World Wars) from 1761.

• In the 19th century, many British families spent time in India, for whose records see p. 147.

Case history

Kylie Minogue's Welsh roots

Although born and bred in Melbourne, Australia, singing sensation and ex-*Neighbours* star Kylie Minogue has roots planted firmly in the Welsh valleys. Her maternal grandmother Millicent Riddiford was born in 1919 at Maesteg, in the Llynfi Valley, Glamorganshire. Millicent's parents were George Riddiford, a coal-hewer who had migrated to the Welsh coalfields from Gloucestershire, and his wife Megan, daughter of Elias Hughes, a slate miner of Blaenau Festiniog. I found from Elias's General Registration birth certificate that he was born on 4 January 1860 at Tanyffordd, Llandderfel near Bala, Merionethshire, son of Moses Hughes, a labourer, and his wife Elizabeth Hughes formerly Evans.

It was then a question of searching back through the General Registration marriage indexes to find a reference to a Moses Hughes that cross-referenced exactly with an Elizabeth Evans. The resulting marriage certificate shows that they walked up the aisle of the Calvanistic Methodist chapel in Bala on 13 May 1857 to marry, before witnesses John Evans and Edward Hughes. Moses was 23, a bachelor and labourer of Nant yr Hefla, Llanycil, son of an earlier Elias Hughes, a farmer.

I later found that the Hugheses had been farmers in Llanasa, Flintshire, since at least the late 18th century. Sadly, the records could not tell me one thing I really wanted to know – could they sing?

bride and groom. Death indexes give ages from 1868,
dates of birth from 1969 and mothers' maiden
names from 1974. Death certificates from 1861 state
(though sometimes inaccurately) the name of the
spouse and the parents' names – a fantastic
resource for tracing further back.

Irish General Registration for Protestant marriages
started on 1 April 1845, and for all births, marriages
and deaths on 1 January 1864. The records and
registration districts are organized as in England and
Wales. Records are held by the Registrar General of
Eire. Northern Ireland split off in 1922 and its records
are with the Registrar General of Northern Ireland,
who also has microfiche copies of most of the pre-
1922 Dublin indexes. Although plans are afoot, the
records are not yet online, except for the indexes to
births 1865–74 and Protestant marriages 1847–64 at
www.familysearch.org. If you know when a post-
1922 Northern Irish event took place you can order
the certificate at www.groni.gov.uk.

want to know more?
• J.G. Ryan's *Irish*
Records: Sources for
Family and Local History
(Ancestry, rev. edn 1997)
goes into detail on all
aspects of Irish records.
• **A good general guide
to General Registration
worldwide is T.J. Kemp's**
International Vital
Records Handbook (4th
edn, Genealogical
Publishing Co., 2001)
• **Most contact details
for General Registration
around the world can
be found at**
www.cyndislist.org.

4 Tracing further back

There are many sources for expanding your family history in the 19th and 20th centuries, and which you can also bring into play if you get stuck using censuses and births, marriages and deaths. We will look at these later. But assuming you've now successfully got back to the 1841 census and the start of General Registration (1837), you'll be burning to go back yet further. Parish registers, wills and manorial records are used to trace information from before these years.

Parish registers

Parish registers that are accessible for research date from 1538 and consist of records of baptisms, marriages and burials made by the local parish. Family historians turn to parish registers when they have gone back as far as they can through General Registration and census returns.

must know

Parish Register indexes

If your family stayed in the same place, and all their events were recorded in registers that have been indexed, you may be able to piece together a skeleton family tree going back to the 16th century. What's more, even if your ancestors moved about quite a lot, you may still be able to find their events taking place in different parishes.

Seeking parish register entries

The best first steps for seeking parish register entries are the International Genealogical Index (IGI), www.familysearch.org and http://freereg.rootsweb.com/. These are indexes to many baptism and marriage registers going right back to when they started, 1538.

Thomas Cromwell was the creator of the parish register and thus a poshumous hero of family historians.

Using www.familysearch.org

Start by keying in the name you want, with or without places or dates, and the site will give you results from a number of indexes, including:

• **Ancestral File:** a compilation from unverified family history information submitted since 1978. Entries include contact details for the submitters, who you can contact for more information.

• **Vital Records Index:** an index of over 4,000,000 parish register entries not on the IGI (International Genealogical Index) and also the majority of births recorded at Dr Williams' Library (www.dwlib.co.uk) and the Wesleyan Methodist Registry, Irish Quaker births and marriages 1850-75, Irish civil registration for births 1865-74 and Protestant marriages 1847-64.

• **Pedigree resource file** containing names, family relationships and birth, marriage and death information for millions of people, appearing as it was originally submitted and not formatted or merged with information submitted by others.

• **Genealogical websites** linked to Familysearch.

• **The International Genealogical Index** itself.

The IGI is the greatest parish register index in the world. It covers mainly Anglican baptism and marriage registers. It doesn't tell you if the registers contained gaps, nor what registers it doesn't include – Kent, for example, is very poorly covered. The indexes at the back of *The Phillimore Atlas and Index of Parish Registers* (Phillimore, rev. edn, 2003) give an idea of coverage, but there is no definitive source.

In the index, C = christening, M = marriage, S = spouse, A = adult baptism and Infant = infant burial (it's usually a guess, not a definite statement of fact, that a recorded infant burial relates to a particular baptism entry). Entries labelled 'Abt' (= About) are normally taken from secondary sources and should be treated gingerly: you may be hindered as well as helped by other people's submissions. Never forget that this is just an index that is intended to lead you to the correct original records.

Original entries in the IGI are accompanied by Batch, Source, Call and Print out Call numbers. You can click on these to see the full catalogue details and, if you wish, to order a copy of the relevant entry or microfilm from your nearest Family History Centre, which you can in turn seek simply by clicking on the hyperlink on the 'Advice' page.

The site http://tinyurl.com/8dkr can be used to obtain a list from IGI data of all entries for a surname that has been extracted from specific parishes. Find your parish, select the batch you want and click on it. Enter the relevant surname in the top right box, and press 'submit query' and the entries will appear.

Record offices

A combination of the censuses and, if you're fortunate, parish register indexes will tell you where your ancestors who were alive in the early-mid 19th century were born and baptised. You can then examine the relevant parish registers. A few of these are still with the churches where they were made, but most are deposited in county record offices or archives. You can locate them by using *The Phillimore Atlas and Index of Parish Registers* (see p. 53), which also includes indispensable maps of each county showing the parish boundaries, and www.a2a.org.uk (or www.scan.org.uk in Scotland), which gives contact details for archives and allows you to access many of their catalogues.

Having established which archive you need, check opening times and booking requirements, and the identification you are required to have with you. Take a pencil, as pens can harm original records. Besides parish registers, you'll find a plethora of other wonderful local sources that will help you, the best of which we'll discuss later. If it's too far for you to travel to a record office, hire a genealogist to go for you, or you can order microfiche copies at your local Mormon Family History Centre.

Useful tip

The Society of Genealogists holds a large collection of transcriptions of original parish registers. These vary in quality depending on who made them, but can still be immensely useful.

Hiring genealogists

There are a growing number of genealogists and record agents available for hire. Genealogists (such as myself) generally charge higher fees and organize and implement all aspects of tracing family trees. Record agents charge less and work to their clients' specific instructions – for example, 'please search the parish registers of X for the period 1730 to 1790 for baptisms, marriage and burials, for anyone of the surname Smiggins'. Most archives have a list of people who work locally or offer their own search services. Many people advertise at the back of genealogy magazines or at sites such as www.genealogypro.com, www.expertgenealogy .com and www.cyndislist.org. The vast majority are trustworthy, and many are very good, but ability varies a great deal. As a rule of thumb, the more prompt and professional their response, and the better presented their results, the more likely they are to be worth their salt. Generally, there is much to be said for utilizing their local expertise.

The parish and its registers

Historically, England and Wales were divided into about 11,000 parishes. You can learn more about these at www.visionofbritain.org.uk and www.genuki.org.uk. Henry VIII decreed that each parish should keep registers of the baptisms, mar- riages and burials of its inhabitants from 1538 onwards. In reality, few survive before 1558, when they started being kept on sheepskin instead of paper, and even then few survive before the 1600s.

From 1598, annual copies were made and sent to the local bishop (to determine which, see

A selection of family history magazines.

www.genuki.org.uk). Called 'Bishops' Transcripts' (or
'Register Bills' in East Anglia), these make a good
substitute for lost original records, and occasionally
contain information omitted from the registers
themselves. They are also in county record offices
and a guide is J. Gibson's *Bishops' Transcripts and
Marriage License Bonds and Allegations: A Guide to
their Location and Indexes* (FFHS, 4th edn, 1997).

Many first-time researchers are disappointed to
find that parish registers are less detailed than
General Registration records. This is true, but just be
grateful they're there at all – our records are among
the very best in the world in terms of detail, survival
and accessibility. In fact, parish registers provide a
fantastic opportunity to find out about your
ancestors' baptisms, marriages and burials in the
years before censuses and General Registration, and
if you need further co-ordinates you can turn to
manorial records and wills (see pages 66–77).

An original baptism certificate
issued by the incumbent of St
Mary, Newington. Such
documents sometimes turn
up in family papers.

Baptisms
The parish register baptism records sometimes
include birth dates, but more usually only the date of
the christening. Baptism may have taken place in the
case of sick babies on the day of the birth, but was

more usually several days, weeks, months or – please take note – years after the event. Early baptism registers sometimes just state the child's name, but certainly from the 17th century onwards they generally give the father's full name, occasionally with details of residence and occupation (this became standard under Rose's Act of 1812). Up to 1812, you'll sometimes find all sorts of juicy details that the clergyman chose to write down. With notable exceptions in the period 1780–1812, usually just the mother's Christian name is given, not her maiden surname – to find this you must seek the couple's marriage records.

Marriages

Before 1754, marriage registers gave the date, the christian names and surnames of both parties, and whatever additional information the clergyman felt inclined to record. For example, at Seasalter, Kent, there's an amusing entry:

'Little Osiah Oakham and Sarah Slater, both of Seasalter, were married by License, September 27 1744. Sarah was his first wife's sister... and now very pregnant'.

Hardwicke's Marriage Act of 25 March 1754 required marriages to be conducted by Anglican clergymen in (with certain exceptions) the home parish of the bride or groom, either after banns had been read in both parties' home parishes for three Sundays running (see p. 58), or on production of a marriage licence.

(see p. 58)

watch out!
Never simply assume that a baptism date was a birth date: record it on your family tree as 'bpt', as opposed to 'b' for 'born'.

Many couples opted for less conventional forms of marriage as depicted in *The Elopement* by George Morland (1763–1804).

Only Jews and Quakers were exempt from this and could marry in their own religious ceremonies. As before, boys could still marry at 14 and girls at 12, but parental consent was required for all under 21.

It was recorded whether the parties were 'bach[elor]' 'spin[ster]' or 'wid[ow/er]', whether banns or a licence were used, the parish of residence ('otp' means 'of this parish' and 'soj[ourner]' refers to someone who had only recently settled there). Both parties had to sign or, if illiterate, make their marks. There were two witnesses, who were often siblings or other relatives of the bride and groom.

watch out!

Don't assume marriage witnesses were related to the bride and groom. Some weddings in the parish had a professional witness besides any relatives who may or may not have also witnessed the event.

Banns or licence?

The reading or 'calling' of banns was a means of preventing bigamy or clandestine marriages, dating back to 1215. Banns were either recorded in the same register as marriages, or in a separate banns book that you'll find with the registers in the record office. They may state the parishes of residence of both parties, so they can lead you from the groom's parish to the one in which he married and vice versa.

Marriage licences originated in the 14th century and enabled marriages to take place immediately – handy if the girl was heavily pregnant, but more usually obtained as status symbols. Usually, if both parties lived in the same bishopric, the licence would be issued by the local bishop – to determine which see www.genuki.org.uk, or look at the maps in *The Phillimore Atlas* (see p. 53) – and the records will be in the relevant record office. If the bride and groom lived in different dioceses within the same archdiocese, licences were issued by the relevant Vicar General in either Canterbury (for the south) and York (for the north). If in doubt consult J. Gibson's *Bishops' Transcripts and Marriage Licenses, Bonds and Allegations* (see p. 56).

Marriage licences add helpful details to the family tree, such as who – usually a close relative – put up the bond. A bond was a statement of a sum of money to be forfeited if the couple were found to be lying about their legal right to marry. Very occasionally the bride's father's name was stated. The site www.englishorigins.net has an index to marriage licence allegations 1694–1850 containing some 670,000 names.

Burials

Early burial registers may just give names, but increasingly as the 17th century progresses you'll find age, residence, occupation and marital status. Children's burials were often accompanied by the father's name. After Rose's Act of 1812, all that was recorded was date, name, residence and age.

Overcoming problems

Parish registers don't always provide enough detail to be able to tell different people of the same name apart and thus to construct a precise family tree. If in doubt, try to gain further co-ordinates on the people concerned using other types of record, such as manorial records and wills.

In Welsh parish registers from the mid-19th century back, you may not be able to find your ancestors' baptisms under the surname you expect. This is often because, instead of hereditary surnames, the Welsh were still employing patronymic surnames that changed from generation to generation. Thus, William Edwards might actually have been baptised as William, son of Edward, and Edward's surname would in turn have been whatever his father had been called. For more about names, see chapter 10.

Generally, if the entry you want isn't in the parish register, go back to the indexes. Besides the main ones already mentioned, there are a great many other indexes that can help you search for original entries in parish registers. *Boyd's Marriage Index*, searchable at www.englishorigins.net, covers about 15 per cent of all pre-1837 marriage registers. *The Pallot Marriage and Baptism Indexes*, searchable at

> **must know**
>
> **Infant mortality**
> Because of high infant mortality (the average was 150 deaths for every 1,000 live births), you can never assume that a baptism you've found is that of your ancestor before you've made a thorough search of the burial registers for at least five years after the baptism (note that the IGI does not include records of burials).

www.ancestry.com, cover the period 1780 to 1837, mainly (but not exclusively) for London and its environs, and contain some entries from registers that were destroyed in the Blitz. Many counties have partial or complete marriage indexes as detailed in *Marriage and Census Indexes for Family Historians* by J. Gibson and E. Hampson (FFHS, 2000): despite all the advances in computer technology, these old indexes still come up trumps time and time again. Notable among burial indexes are *Boyd's London Burials*, covering some 250,000 burials of adult males in London from 1538 to 1853, at www.Englishorigins.com, and *The National Burial Index*, available at many libraries and from the Federation of Family History Societies on CD-ROM.

Ultimately, if all index searches fail, you may simply have to list the parishes surrounding your home parish and search their registers manually, and if that fails search in those surrounding *them*, and so on. Intelligent guesses can be made by working out where the local market was and searching the registers of the parishes surrounding it.

Scotland and Ireland

John Knox made Presbyterianism the most widespread form of Christianity in Scotland in the 1560s. By the 1637 Covenant, it became Scotland's established church. All its surviving parish registers, called 'Old Parochial Registers', are indexed at www.scotlandspeople.gov.uk; the originals are with the Registrar General of Scotland at New Register House. Maps showing the location of Scotland's parishes (there are approximately 900) are included in *The Phillimore Atlas*.

The drawbacks are:
- Few registers survive from before the mid-18th century.
- There are no Bishops' Transcripts.
- There were virtually no burials recorded.
- Many marriages were common-law ones (called 'handfasting' or 'hamfesting') that were never recorded.

Pluses include:
- Women's maiden names were usually recorded in burials and in the baptisms of their children.
- Birth records often include godparents' names.
- The local kirk sessions (the records of the parish's administration: see www.scan.org. uk) often record 'mort cloth dues' – the records of renting out the parish's black pall to cover the coffin, that tell you the date of the burial and the deceased's name.

Many non-Presbyterian church registers appear in www.familysearch.org and the originals are usually either in the National Archives of Scotland or still with the chapels where they were made.

For Ireland, few (Protestant) Church of Ireland registers survived the IRA bombing in 1922. Early Irish Catholic records are equally thin on the ground: Catholicism was not fully legalized in Ireland until 1829 and few Catholic priests dared keep registers before then (see pages 142–4 for more information).

must know
Bridge the gap
The absence of your ancestor's baptism in the period 1642-9 and 1649-60 could well be because it simply was not recorded. Sources such as wills, manorial records and so on can often be used to bridge the gap.

Civil War records

The English Civil War (1642-9) and Interregnum (1649-60) caused a break in records such as parish registers, called the 'Commonwealth Gap'. Luckily, there are plenty of other records generated at the time that can be used to bridge it.

● During the Civil War and Interregnum many Anglican clergymen were 'ejected' from their parishes by Parliament, and replaced with Presbyterian clergy, only to be thrown out in turn in favour of the original incumbents when the king was restored in 1660. The Presbyterians did not maintain the parish registers – hence the Commonwealth Gap. They kept a system of civil registration of births, marriages and deaths instead, but very few of these records have survived.

● Ship Money – the raising of which by Charles I was a major cause of the outbreak of Civil War between him and Parliament – was levied between 1634 and 1640, with records in the National Archives (series SP 16 and SP 17).

● In 1642, in the run-up to war, Parliament demanded an oath of the English, called the 'Protestation', that pledged loyalty to the King *and* Parliament. The resulting lists made in each parish (some of which have survived) show which adult males swore and who refused – a useful mini-census that pinpoints people in their home villages before the disruption that was to follow. Many of those published by county record societies are at the House of Lords Record Office. They are catalogued in *The Protestation Returns 1641–42 and Other Contemporary Listings: Collection in Aid of Distressed Protestants in Ireland, Subsidies, Poll tax,*

Charles I in Three positions, painting by Carlo Maratta after Van Dyck (1625–1713).

Assessments or Grants, Vow and Covenant, Solemn League and Covenant by J. Gibson and A. Dell (FFHS, 1995). As you can see, this also includes other useful contemporary lists, such as the round of oath swearing known as the 'Solemn League and Covenant', a national pledge to adopt Presbyterianism in order to secure Parliament the help of the Scots in 1643/4.

• Officers and some soldiers on both sides of the Civil War are in paylists and musters in the National Archives, best accessed in print using *The Regimental History of Cromwell's Army* by Sir C. Firth and G. Davies (Clarendon Press, 1940), E. Peacock's *The Army Lists of the Roundheads and Cavaliers* (Chatto & Windus, 2nd edn, 1874) and S. Reid's *Officers and Regiments of the Royalist Army* (Partizan Press, n.d.).

• Charles I was captured in 1646 and executed in January 1649. Two great sets of records, abstracted and indexed by Mary Anne Everett Green in the late 19th century, cover Parliaments' financial dealings with the defeated Royalists and provide much detail about them and their sufferings. These are the *Calendar of the Proceedings of the Committee for Advance of Money, 1642–56, preserved in the State Paper Office of Her Majesty's Public Record Office* (1888) and *Calendar of the Proceedings of the Committee for Compounding, etc, 1643–60, preserved in the State Paper Office of Her Majesty's Public Record Office* (1889–92).

• Charles II was restored in 1660. The 'Free and Voluntary Present' of 1661 (which was really nothing of the sort) created a tax list of 130,000 of the better-off Englishmen, usually with occupations, in National Archives series E 179. It started a series of useful round-ups showing where people ended up in the period after the conflict. Of these the best are the Hearth Tax Returns of 1662–89, a tax on the fireplaces of all but the very poor (and those such as bakers who used hearths for work). They are catalogued at http://www.nationalarchives. gov.uk/e179/ and in J. Gibson's *The Hearth Tax, and Other Later Stuart Tax Lists and the Association Rolls* (FFHS, 2nd edn, 1996), which also indicates what's in county record offices and what's been published. Scottish hearth taxes for 1661–94 are at the National Archives of Scotland. Surviving returns for Ireland, called 'Hearth Money Rolls', are listed in J.G. Ryan's *Irish Records: Sources for Family and Local History* (Ancestry, rev. edn, 1997), and those for Dublin are on www.irishfamilyresearch.co.uk.

A hearth tax return from 1664.

Case history

David Jason's Wealden roots

Actor Sir David Jason has such a distinctive London accent, and is so closely associated with his on-screen role of Londoner Del Boy in *Only Fools and Horses*, that I was surprised to find from the censuses that his great-grandfather Henry lived in Lancashire, but was born in 1851 in Sussex.

The family surname was White – David took 'Jason' as a stage name – and Henry White's father, James White, was born about 1826 in neighbouring Chiddingly, son of an earlier Henry White. This was before General Registration started (1837) so I sought him in the Chiddingly parish registers, deposited at the East Sussex Record Office, where I found the following entry:

5 Nov 1826 James s. Henry & Dinah White of Chiddingly labourer

This couple had twelve children in all, starting with Stephen, baptised in 1808. The marriage of Henry and Dinah appeared in the Chiddingly marriage registers, thus:

29 Aug 1807 Henry White of this parish bach[elor] & Dinah Guy X of the same, spin[ster]. Witnesses Wm Duplock X, Francis Guy X and Jas. Potter

'X' indicates a mark made instead of a signature. Francis Guy was a relation of Dinah's, but James Potter was a regular witness at many Chiddingly weddings and was not related. Subsequent research showed that the Whites and Guys were prolific Chiddingly families, who farmed and made bricks from the local Wealden clay. The vestry book, in the Chiddingly parish chest and now also at the Record Office, showed that when Dinah fell ill in 1832, the parish gave Henry five shillings for a nurse to attend her, and when she died they paid for her funeral. Because Dinah had died, several of their younger children had to go into the workhouse. No wonder their descendants later sought work in the industrial north, and then in London.

Wills

Wills are a fantastic source for tracing back even further than parish registers and, if you're very lucky, into the Middle Ages. They are also important for your research down to the present. At any point if you get stuck, or need proof that someone was an ancestor, wills can provide much needed extra co-ordinates.

must know

Leaving legacies

Wills are written by people to express how they wish their property and money to be inherited when they die. Because people usually leave legacies to close family, they are immensely useful to genealogists wishing to learn about, and prove, family relationships.

Wills and administrations

Wills can sometimes enable us to trace family trees in their own right, but they are most often used to clarify and prove pedigrees constructed from General Registration records, censuses and parish registers. They also provide colour by detailing unusual belongings, eccentric desires and suggesting how members of the family felt about each other.

You may find the will of someone who you think could be your ancestor. Hopefully, they will name their children, thus confirming the relationships. They may also name their spouse, siblings, nieces and nephews, and sometimes you may find mention of parents. Bequests to relatives in other places, or (especially in old wills) to churches or the poor of certain parishes, provide strong clues as to where the person may have originated. Witnesses and executors (see below) may well turn out to be relations.

In wills, the testator nominated 'executors', who were usually close relatives or friends, to distribute their property after their death. The executors would take the will to a probate court to 'prove' it, by swearing to its authenticity and undertaking to fulfil its instructions. Wills were usually written by lawyers following their clients' instructions but sometimes they were dictated by testators, usually on their deathbeds: these were called 'nuncupative wills'. If no will was made, the deceased was said to be 'intestate'. The estate could be wound up privately, or a close relative or friend might visit a probate court and apply for 'letters of administration' to authorize them to do so. Such administrations (or 'admons') are far less useful than wills but still provide a few helpful details such as the intestate's occupation and the administrator's relationship to the deceased.

A Dying Man Dictating his Will (14th century). **Many deaths, even from the Middle Ages, were followed by the proving of wills.**

Wills may also nominate supervisors or 'overseers', to supplement the work of the executors, and who were also usually trusted relatives or friends. At the end of the will you may find one or more 'codicils', which were later additions that modified parts of the will, made, for example, after a spouse had died or a new child had been born.

Where to search: after 1858

From 12 January 1858, all wills and administrations were handled by the Principal Probate Registry (PPR),

Who could write wills?

Generally, the wealthier the person, the more likely they were to have written a will, but some rich people omitted to do so. There are, moreover, many wills for tradesmen and labourers, even some for paupers.
- Until 1837, men could write wills from 14 years old and women from 12.
- Until 1882, wives' property technically belonged to their husbands, so it is very rare to find a testatrix (i.e. a female testator) who was not a spinster or a widow.

must know

Proved when?

Wills were often proved straight after someone died, but they could be proved a year or several years later. Sometimes you find a husband's will not being proved until his widow died many years later, so a wide search sometimes pays off.

which used to be at Somerset House but has now been demoted to less glamorous surroundings nearby at First Avenue House and renamed the Principal Registry of the Family Division. The indexes up to 1943 are available on microfiche at many archives and Mormon Family History Centres, but thereafter you need to search at First Avenue House in person, pay the PPR's Postal Searches and Copies Department to search for you or hire a genealogist. The indexes state helpful details including the name and residence of the deceased, date of death, executors and administrators, and their addresses. As they are arranged annually, they are much easier to search than General Registration death indexes, though of course far fewer people appear.

Where to search: before 1858

Old original wills are sometimes found in family papers, but usually you will encounter the probate copies that were made by clerks in the probate court. Wills were proved (and administrations granted) in church (or 'ecclesiastical') courts controlled by the local bishop or archdeacon. *The Phillimore Atlas* (see p. 53) and www.genuki.org.uk show the jurisdictions – often archdeaconries – that covered the parishes. If the deceased had property in more than one ecclesiastical jurisdiction, or the family had the social pretension to be the sort of people who might, the will could be proved in the next most senior court – usually the local bishop's – rising, ultimately, to the Prerogative Courts [of the Archbishops] of York and Canterbury, whose will indexes include people (usually of the wealthier sort) from all over the realm. The latter also includes anyone who had money in the Bank of England or who died abroad ('in foreign parts', often abbreviated to 'pts'), including soldiers and sailors. Between the years 1653 and 1660, under the Cromwellian regime, all wills in England and Wales were proved at the Prerogative Court of Canterbury (PCC).

This sounds complicated, but usually it isn't. You'll quickly find the local will indexes, either manuscript or published, at the county record office and if you have problems you can also consult *Probate Jurisdictions: Where to Look for Wills* by J. Gibson and E. Churchill (FFHS, 5th edn, 2002). Most Welsh wills are at the National Library of Wales. Those for York are at the Borthwick Institute and are largely covered by published indexes. All wills proved at the PCC are indexed at www.documentsonline.nationalarchives.gov.uk where you can download copies of the documents.

A late 17th-century will, complete with signature and marks.

must know
Will abstracts
A scan of the record office's shelves will show you that some wills have been published in the form of abstracts, that is, cutting out the legal jargon and providing the salient details. Abstracts provide more than enough detail for tracing ancestry, but be aware that they are secondary sources and you may need to check the originals.

You may also find other documentation in the form of probate acts, which record such things as the appointment of new executors if the original ones died or couldn't be bothered, and 'inventories'. Inventories were compiled especially in the 16th and 17th centuries and are either to be found with the will or indexed separately at the archives. They are always worth seeking as they comprise lists of the deceased's goods and chattels, with their value, sometimes right down to their clothes, books and farming implements.

Things to bear in mind

The will indexes, if you're lucky, will reveal not only the person you are looking for, but also others of the same name who may be related.

- You must, as in all genealogical research, think of and seek variant spellings.
- Don't be put off by the legal jargon or imagine this was how your ancestor actually spoke – when the will of a farmer states, 'I devise and bequeath unto my eldest son Thomas my black coat', he probably said, 'and I want Tommy to have this 'ere coat'.
- You only need to note the main points and thus make what are called 'genealogical abstracts' – names, relationships, what they were to have.
- Don't worry about repetitive clauses stating what was to happen if various eventualities happened, as they seldom did.

- Don't just search wills for the surname line: look for wills of the wives' and in-laws' families, as these may include bequests to members of your direct line.

West Country wills

Sadly, most pre-1858 Cornwall, Devon and Somerset wills were lost in Second World War bombing, but the indexes remain and the Devon Record Office has a collection of abstracts made of some of them before they were lost. Wills of West Country people in the Estate Duty series (see p. 72) and PCC were unaffected.

Wills in Scotland and Ireland

Until 1868, land descended strictly to the next legal heir – father to son, and so on – so the only thing Scots could bequeath was moveable property and money. They did so using 'testaments' (technically, a will only bequeaths land, but in England the term has

Useful tip

If you're dealing with a small village and are stuck, a random search of wills for anyone living there might reveal chance bequests to your ancestors that can provide vital clues from hitherto unsuspected relationships.

come to cover both land and other property). Testaments are kept at the National Archives of Scotland, and a growing index to them, for 1531–1901, is at www.scotlandspeople.gov.uk. You can also look in 'Services to Heirs' (also called 'retours') that recorded the passing of land from a deceased land-holder to an heir who was not their child, covering cases where land passed from a childless man to a niece or nephew, for example, and providing many fascinating family relationships. The records for 1700–1859 are indexed in printed volumes available at good libraries and on CD-ROM from the Scottish Genealogical Society.

Irish wills after 1922 are divided between the National Archives in Dublin and the Public Record Office of Northern Ireland. Those before 1922 were mostly destroyed when the IRA bombed the Four Courts in Dublin that year. The survivals include the indexes, some of the documents, locally made copies from 1858 onwards and collections of

Estate Duty and Bank of England wills

From 1796 to 1903 many wills were abstracted in Estate Duty registers. Their indexes at the National Archives in series IR 27 have the advantage, before 1858, of covering wills from all ecclesiastical courts, thus making the searches for 'missing' wills much easier. These abstracts are interesting because they show how money was actually distributed among beneficiaries (wills merely state what was intended). There is an index online at www.nationalarchivist.com, though it is rather difficult to use.

Similar abstracts for estates including government stocks, covering 1717 to 1845, are held in the Bank of England Archive Section, Threadneedle Street, London, EC2R 8AH, 0207 601 5096, www.bankofengland.co.uk/archive.htm, and indexed at www.Englishorigins.net.

abstracts of wills made before then. They can be examined at the National Archives in Dublin and the Public Record Office of Northern Ireland. See also P.B. Eustace's *Registry of Deeds, Dublin, Abstracts of Wills* (Irish Manuscripts Commission, 1954–84), which contains much of interest, albeit for the better-off sort. If you're dealing with poor Catholic families, the loss of Ireland's wills makes little difference, as very few made wills in the first place.

The bombing of the Four Courts in Dublin in 1922 destroyed most Irish court records, wills and many Protestant parish registers. However, some records survived - and they are still available to be searched!

Manorial records

Like wills, manorial records can help you trace back into the Middle Ages. They can also help solve problems at any point between then and 1922, when the manorial record system was abolished, or be searched simply to give colour to an existing family tree.

Manors and their records

Manors are units of land usually comprising a village and its farm and common land. The earliest manors have their roots in villages that pre-dated Roman times. Some others are derived from Roman estates established in the first couple of centuries AD . They became the basic unit of land-holding under William the Conqueror. Parishes developed out of them, and from the 16th century took over many of the local administrative functions formerly exercised by manors. While parish boundaries remained largely static, manorial borders chopped and changed as lords amalgamated, swapped and sold bits of land, so some ended up no bigger than tiny farms and others were much larger – the Yorkshire manor of Wakefield covered 150 square miles.

Manors were administered by the lord's steward, who managed the manor, with a bailiff to collect rents, a reeve to collect fines, a hayward to maintain the infrastructure of fences, barns and so forth, and a constable to keep law and order and see off vermin.

Manorial tenants may be found in all manner of manorial records, not least as jurors. The best records, though, are those of the Court Baron (or 'Halmote'). Manorial tenants had obligations to fulfil,

either by labour or surrender of produce or money, but their possession of their ancestral tenancies was guaranteed by inviolable rights. These obligations and rights were recorded in the Court Rolls. When someone became a tenant, whether by inheritance or purchase, they would be given a copy of these obligations and rights, and were thus known as 'copyholders'. When a tenant died their heir would appear at the next Court Baron and state their right to inherit the tenancy. They would then have their right acknowledged, thus being 'admitted' to the copyholding, and paying a forfeit to do so. The forfeit was traditionally a 'heriot', the tenant's best beast, but after the Restoration (1660) a money payment was made instead.

Richmond Castle, Yorkshire, by Alexander Keirincx (1600-c.52). Until 1922, all of England's green and pleasant land was subdivided into manors.

must know
Accurate records
Creating manorial
records involved
presenting evidence
before the local
community, so any
accidental mistakes
could be contradicted
by those listening, and
hoodwinking others
was virtually
impossible. Manorial
records are more likely
to be accurate than
practically any other
records you will
encounter in your
research.

Even when written in Latin, as they usually were
before 1732, the records are often quite easy to search
for the surnames you want. You can have a go at
tackling the Latin yourself using the guide on page 79,
but otherwise, do not fear – Latin translators are not
too expensive!

Where to search

One of the main purposes in setting up county
record offices was to preserve manorial records
after the system was abolished in 1922. Many will
be there. However, a good number of manors were
owned by people or institutions, such as universities,
located in other counties, so the records may be
found in a record office far removed from the

In the Middle Ages, most people
were tied to the land under the
manorial system.

county in which the manor was situated. *The Manorial Documents Register* of the Historic Manuscripts Commission identifies the whereabouts of a great many records. It's at the National Archives and is being slowly transferred on to www.nationalarchives.gov.uk/mdr.

Many owners held on to their records, so if all else fails you may need to identify the pre-1922 owner using directories (see p. 91) and then trace their heirs today, for which purpose *Burke's Peerage* and *Burke's Landed Gentry* (see p. 165) are often helpful.

Interpreting the records

There are several excellent guides to manorial records and how to interpret them, including:

- J. West's *Village Records* (Phillimore, rev. edn, 1997)
- P. Palgrave-Moore's *How to Locate and Use Manorial Records* (Elvery Dowers, 1985)
- D. Stuart's *Manorial Records: An Introduction to their Transcription and Translation* (Phillimore, 1992).

Useful tip

Unlike the manorial system of landholding they controlled, the Lordships of Manors were not abolished in 1922. Some manorial lords now belong to The Manorial Society, which organizes auctions of these titles and can be helpful in tracking down manorial records too.

Genealogy survival kit

For those new to genealogical research, some of the practices and terms used – especially in the earlier records – can seem daunting. This section provides some miscellaneous basic facts relevant to researching ancestry and which you may need to look up as you trace your family tree.

Old words
Specialist dictionaries like R. Milward's *A Glossary of Household, Farming and Trade Terms from Probate Inventories* (Derbyshire Record Society, occasional paper 1, various edns) and the *Oxford English Dictionary* will de-code the archaic words you encounter.

Old handwriting

Reading old handwriting is called palaeography. In the past, some letters were written differently from the way they are now, so are extremely unfamiliar.

For example, 'e' was often written *ℓ* ℯ *e* *ε* *℮*

'c' as *cr* *D* *ϕ* *φ*

's' as *ſ* ℯ *6* *8* *ß* and so on.

H. Marshall's *Palaeography for Family and Local Historians* (Phillimore, 2004) is an excellent guide. A free course in English palaeography, 1500–1700, is at www.english.cam.ac.uk/ceres/ehoc.index.html.

You can often work out what letters were. For example, if you can read 'Ed-ard' then you can surmise the other letter is a 'w'. You can also see how letters were written in phrases or words that are legible – many wills, for example, will start 'In the name of God Amen', so you can see how the scribe wrote his 'I's, 'n's, 't's and so on before tackling the will itself.

Writers often abbreviated words using apostrophes, or apostrophes followed by the last letters.

Sometimes the apostrophes were just missed out. 'William' was often written 'Will'm' or 'Wm', 'James' as 'Jas', 'Majesty' as 'Maty' and so on.

Latin

Few things terrify genealogists as much as the use of Latin in old records. If you really can't cope with basic Latin there are some very good, modestly priced translators.

E.A. Gooder's *Latin for Local History: An Introduction* (Longmann, 2nd edn, 1978) and R.A. Latham's *Revised Medieval Latin Word-list from British and Irish Sources* (OUP, 1965) are very useful guides. There is an online guide at www.genuki.org.uk.

Here are some basics:

annus	year
dies	day
est	is
filia	daughter
filius	son
mater	mother
matrimonium	married
mensis	month
mortuus	died
natus	born
nuptium	married
obit	died
parochia	parish
pater	father
sepultat	buried
uxor	wife
vidua	widow

The beginning of St Luke's Gospel, Lindisfarne Gospels, c.698, presents Latin palaeography somewhat earlier than most genealogists will encounter.

Money

The pre-decimal currency was pounds ('l' = livres), shillings ('s') and pence ('d' = dinarii). Four pounds, two shillings and three pence ('thruppence') could be written £4-2-3 or £4 2s 3d or 4l 2s 3d or – using Roman numerals – ivl iis iiid or even iiijl ijs iijd.

It's very difficult to find out how much money was worth relative to its value today. The Bank of England has a ready reckoner, and you can also study C.R. Chapman's *How Heavy, How Much and How Long? Weights, Money and Other Measures Used by Our Ancestors* (Lochin Publishing, 1995) and L. Mumby's *How Much is that Worth?* (Phillimore for BALH, rev. edn, 1996).

Dates

Years and days haven't always been recorded the same way in every country. See C.R. Cheney (ed.), *Handbook of Dates for Students of English History* (rev. edn, M. Jones, CUP, 2000) for lists of all old forms of dating, including by saints' days (e.g. St George's Day 1660 was 23 April 1660) and popes' and kings' regnal years. Years were often counted from the date of a sovereign's accession, so for example '1 Elizabeth II' represents the first year of the reign of Elizabeth II, which started on 6 February 1952, the day she succeeded her father; the year '53 Elizabeth II' started on 6 February 2004 and ended on 5 February 2005. Cheney also provides a calendar for looking up which day of the week fell on what date in a given year, so if someone wrote a letter dated 25 May 1657 saying their father died 'last Monday' you can find out that 25 May 1657 was a Friday, so 'last Monday' was 20 May.

New and old style

Britain and Europe used to use the Julian calendar, whereby the year began on Lady Day, 25 March, not the Gregorian calendar introduced by the Pope in 1582, which starts the year on 1 January. The Julian calendar began to die out among lay people in the Tudor period, and by the 18th century it is often hard to tell whether a date is being given in 'Old Style' or 'New Style'.

This means that dates appearing in old records need adjusting to make sense in modern terms. A baptism recorded in a parish register on 24 January 1722 would, in modern terms, have taken place on 24 January 1723 because, under the old calendar, New Year's Day (25 March) had not yet arrived. To avoid confusion researchers record the date using 'double dating', giving the old-style year followed by the new-style year, e.g. 24 January 1722/3. On the IGI, dates are allegedly adjusted but without double dating. Nonconformist registers were using new-style dating well in advance of 1752.

Another difference between the old-style Julian and new-style Gregorian calendars was that the latter used leap years but the former didn't. By the time Pope Gregory introduced the new calendar in 1582, the lack of leap years had already caused the old-style date to lapse ten days behind the solar year, so he simply ordered ten days to be cut off 1582, between 4 and 15 October. Because England persisted with the old calendar, it sunk increasingly behind Europe, and was eleven days behind by the 17th century. Therefore, events that share the same dates in different countries, such as the deaths of Shakespeare and Cervantes on 23 April 1616 in

must know

Calendar changes
Different countries changed to the new-style Gregorian calendar from the old-style Julian calendar at different times. Most of Western Europe changed in 1582, Scotland in 1600, England and Wales in 1752 and Russia and the Balkans in the 20th century.

England and Spain respectively, actually took place eleven days apart in real life. England and Wales lost the days between 2 and 14 September 1752 in order to catch up with Europe.

A member of Pope Gregory's commission on the calendar pointing out the backslide of the Julian calendar.

Trends

In the mid-1800s:

- Almost half the population (46 per cent) was under 20 – now it's only 25 per cent.
- An average mid-19th century family had 5 or more children – now the average is 1.7.
- In the mid-19th century, there were 150 deaths for every 1,000 live births; now infant deaths account for only 1 per cent of all deaths.
- Men generally died before 40; now the average is 75.
- In 1848, women dying in childbirth numbered 4 in every 1,000, compared with 6 per 100,000 now.
- A third of deaths were caused by infection – now, cancer accounts for 25 per cent of all deaths.

Societies

Founded in 1911, the Society of Genealogists is a cornerstone of British genealogy, publishing the *Genealogists' Magazine* and maintaining a formidable library of published and manuscript sources at its London base. There are many other family history societies for counties, countries, occupations, religious groups and surnames, including the GOONS ('Guild of One-Name Studies', www.one-name.org). Their umbrella organization is the Federation of Family History Societies (www.ffhs.org.uk). Membership includes many Commonwealth and United States societies too, and it publishes *Family History News and Digest* biannually, summarizing the contents of the different journals.

Family history societies have membership worldwide and their journals include articles on relevant sources and case studies, lists of members' interests and ancestral names. Many also have their own libraries and organize projects to index records such as gravestones and censuses. It's a good idea to join your nearest family history society even if you do not have any local ancestors, because many of the talks will be of more general application, and many organize reciprocal research via societies in other locations.

want to know more?
- *The Family and Local History Handbook* (published by Robert Blatchford) provides a list of archives, societies and other items you will need to trace your family tree.
- An excellent guide to specialist archives of organizations, clubs, businesses and much more is *British Archives: A Guide to Archive Resources in the United Kingdom* by J. Foster and J. Sheppard (Palgrave, 4th edn, 2002).

5 Further sources

Once you've searched the main sources
outlined in previous chapters, there's a rich
store of other archives awaiting that will help
you to fill in the details of your family tree.
These can be used simply to add to your
knowledge of your ancestors and their world, or
to expand your family tree sideways to
encompass more living relatives. They can also
be brought in specifically to gain another set of
co-ordinates on people so as to overcome
problems in tracing and proving their origins.

Beyond the basics

There are many sources besides the main ones already mentioned that can be used to solve problems and to add a huge amount of extra detail to your family's history. The main ones are listed here, alphabetically, and range from adoption records to magazines and newspapers.

watch out!
Pre-1927 adoptions were often informal arrangements with no written records, which may bring your research to a full stop, or mislead you into thinking that a child for whom no birth certificate can be found was the offspring of what were actually foster parents.

Adoption and fostering records

Formal adoption started in 1927. As of January 2006, people trying to seek children adopted out of their family can employ an Intermediary Agency to find them. See www.gro.gov.uk/gro/content/adoptions/ for more details. Adopted children can ask their local Social Services for their original adoption file and birth record; they will be given advice and counselling, and they can start seeking birth relatives using the Adoption Contact Register via the GRO website (above) and the genealogical techniques outlined in this book. In Scotland, both parties can apply for more information to the relevant sheriff's court where the adoption occurred and seek advice from Birthlink. The Adoption Contact Register for Northern Ireland is with the General Register Office, Belfast. For Southern Ireland, contact the Federation of Services for Unmarried Parents and their Children. (See pages 185–8 for contact addresses.)

Before 1927, adoption was occasionally undertaken formally using a solicitor, but was more commonly a completely informal affair, whereby a child was taken in by a family, who may or may not have been relatives, and given their surname. Many arrangements were handled by Dr Barnardo's (founded

1865), who have excellent records but which are stored under the original name only, not the adopted name. Fostering continued after 1927: until 1970 (when the Social Services agency was created) some local authorities kept files on informal fostering. Surviving records are now with Social Services, along with all records from 1970 onwards.

Change of name

Changing surname can be undertaken informally, and often was. More formal name changes, for which you'll sometimes find a deed poll, were usually published in *The Times*, *London Gazette* or a local paper (see page 99). See also *An Index to Changes of Name under Authority of Act of Parliament or Royal License and including Irregular Changes from... 1760 to 1901* by W.P. Phillimore and E.A. Fry (1905, reprinted by GPC 1968).

Adopted children were usually given new surnames so can be very hard to trace.

Court cases

Many ancestors appear in court cases, either as 'plaintiffs', bringing action against others, as 'defendants' (or 'respondents'), answering the charges, or as witnesses or jurors.

Many records of court cases, both criminal and civil, are at the National Archives, whose catalogue, www.catalogue.nationalarchives.gov.uk, indexes an increasing number of them. More are being abstracted and indexed, especially by county record societies, as you will see on the shelves of the county record offices. Trials at the Old Bailey, London, have become a lot easier to find with the launch of www.oldbaileyonline.org, which contains more than 100,000 trials dating from 1674 to 1834.

must know
Court reports
Newspapers (see p. 99)
provide accounts of
court cases that are
often more detailed and
easier to search than
the records of the courts
themselves.

Among the courts you may encounter are those of
Chancery and Exchequer, whose records are partly
indexed on the National Archives website (catalogued
under departments 'C' and 'E' respectively). These
date from the Middle Ages and are mainly concerned
with arguments over money. They thus contain a
vast amount of genealogical information, especially
when disputes were over wills. In fact, the more
quarrelsome your ancestors, the easier they are likely
to be to trace!

So great is the volume of trial records that it will be
many years – if ever – before all are covered by find-aids.
Sadly, the records themselves are simply too massive to
start searching manually unless you've a shrewd idea
that you're going to find something relevant.

Church courts dealt with matters relating to the
church, such as tithe payments, drunken priests,
heresy, witchcraft and morality, but mainly with

House of Lords by T. Rowlandson
(1756–1827) and A.C. Pugin
(1762–1832), the most senior
Court of Appeal until 1875.

sexual misconduct in all its many and varied forms. For this reason they were called the 'bawdy courts'. The records are mainly in county record offices. Appeals against sentences could be made to the Court of Arches (with records at Lambeth Palace Library, indexed in J. Houston's *Cases in the Court of Arches 1660–1913*, BRS vol. 85, 1972) and the Chancery Court of York (records at the Borthwick Institute). Records tend to be in Latin. Some have been translated and published: the record office staff will know what's available for your area.

Details of Scotland's criminal records, most of which are at the National Archives of Scotland, are in C. Sinclair's *Tracing your Scottish Ancestors: A Guide to Ancestry Research in the Scottish Record Office* [the old name for the NAS] (HMSO, rev. edn, 1997). Due to bombing, very little at all survives for Ireland.

Deeds

Deeds record land-holding and transfer. They will often state family relationships, identifying, say, a man and his wife. This is particularly so if you're lucky enough to find a 'lease for lives', a deed designed to run for the lifetimes of three or more named individuals, who were often several generations of the same family. Parties to other deeds may often be related, even if this is not stated. You are most likely to encounter deeds relevant to your ancestry in archives, via the Access to Archives website www.a2a.org.uk and the Historic Manuscripts Commission's National Register of Archives database at www.nationalarchives.gov.uk. Many are also found in the deeds registries for the following specific counties and periods only:

must know

Land registries
The English and Welsh land registry (HM Land Registry) was established in 1862. Its records, though interesting, are generally far less useful for genealogical purposes than deeds. There's a separate Scottish land registry at the Registers of Scotland Executive Agency. Irish deeds from 1708 are at the deeds registry in Dublin.

Middlesex (c.1709-1938) London
Metropolitan Archives, 40 Northampton
Road, London EC1R 0HB, tel: 020 7332 3820,
www.cityoflondon.gov.uk
Bedford Level (1600 onwards) Cambridge
Record Office, Shire Hall, Castle Hill,
Cambridge CB3 0AP, tel: 01480 375842,
www.cambridgeshire.gov.uk
West Riding of Yorkshire (1704-1972)
West Yorkshire Archive Service, Newstead
Road, Wakefield, Yorkshire WF1 2DE, tel:
01924 305980, www.archives.wyjs.org.uk
East Riding and Hull (1708-1976) East
Riding of Yorkshire Archives and Records,
County Hall, Beverley HU17 9BA, tel: 01482
392790, www.eastriding.gov.uk/learning
**North Riding of Yorkshire (not York
itself) (1736-1972)** North Yorkshire County
Record Office, County Hall, Northallerton,
Yorkshire DL7 8AF, tel: 01609 777585,
www.northyorks.gov.uk

A common form of deed, dating from the 1100s to
1833, are 'Feet of Fines'. These are so called
because they were 'final agreements' by which
land was transferred from one party to another,
written in triplicate on a sheet of sheep- or
goatskin divided three ways, the two upper copies
going to the buyer and seller and the bottom copy
or 'foot' enrolled in the Court of Common Pleas.
Surviving copies are kept in the National Archives,
mainly indexed in series IND 1/7233-44 and
1/7217-68. More to the point, many have been

published by county record societies, whose volumes you will find on the shelves of local archives and libraries.

Directories

By searching a series of directories you can build up an idea of when ancestors lived and died, and they also provide addresses for manual searches of censuses. Directories are published lists of people's addresses and occupations that fulfilled broadly the same role as telephone directories do today. They give you a snapshot of the communities in which ancestors lived, including useful historical sketches and descriptions of the places concerned.

Directories started in 1677 as lists of prominent merchants. They proliferated in the 19th century and flourished until the spread of telephone directories (which had actually existed since the 1880s) after the Second World War. They generally listed tradesmen, craftsmen, merchants, professionals, farmers, clergy, gentry and nobility, but as time passed coverage became greater.

Directory sections

From the mid-19th century onwards, directories usually comprised four sections:
• Commercial: listing tradesmen and professionals alphabetically.
• Trades: individual alphabetical lists of tradesmen and professionals arranged under each trade or profession.
• Streets: lists of tradesmen and private residents arranged house by house, street by street.
• Court: originally the heads of wealthier households but this rapidly became simply an alphabetical listing of the heads of all families save the poor.

watch out!

Directories were usually printed a year or so after the information had been collected, so were always slightly out of date.

The best places to find directories are local archives, the Society of Genealogists, online at the University of Leicester's national collection www.historicaldirectories.org/, or on CD-ROM bought from companies such as www.archive cdbooks.org and www.genealogysupplies.com.

Mixed company patronizes a popular London coffee shop near the 'Olympic' theatre, Wych Street, Strand, **by Robert & George Cruilshank, from** *Life in London,* **1820.**

Divorce records

Divorce records from 1943 are at the Principal Registry of the Family Division and will be searched by the staff for £20 per ten years. Those going back to 1858 are in National Archives series J 77 and searchable at www.catalogue.national archives.gov.uk (though few for 1937–43 survive).

Before 1858 you could only divorce by private Act of Parliament, and only 318 couples did so successfully. These (and in fact all Acts of Parliament) are searchable on www.a2a.org.uk. Most couples wanting to separate did so by seeking annulments in church courts (see p. 88). If one party had vanished for seven years the other could remarry with impunity without divorcing. Scottish divorces, which were traditionally much easier to obtain, are at the National Archives of Scotland.

Electoral registers and poll books

Electoral registers have been kept from 1832 and are to be found in local archives (modern ones are on www.192.com). All men aged over 20 could vote from 1918, and all women over 20 from 1928, though before this date some women property holders were eligible. The age requirement was reduced to 18 in 1970. Electoral registers can be used to pin down the span of people's residences at particular addresses, but bear in mind that by the time they were printed they were usually slightly out of date. An appearance and disappearance from an address can be used as a gauge of when someone may have come of age and when they died. Poll books record who could vote, and how they voted, from 1696, and are best sought in local archives. Records are far from comprehensive: voting rights were restricted to men, with decreasingly restrictive age and property requirements.

Gravestones

Also known as 'monumental inscriptions' (MIs), gravestones often give a date of death and age, and may identify other members of the family (whether or not buried in the same grave). In lucky cases, they can provide all sorts of other details about the family, such as parents' names and places of origin. It's always worth visiting the graveyard or cemetery and coming into physical proximity with the earth in which your forebears lie. By doing so, you may well find other gravestones for hitherto unsuspected relatives. Some archives have transcriptions of local MIs and indexes to a few of them are in *Specialist Indexes for Family Historians* by J. Gibson and E. Hampson (FFHS, 1998).

must know

Finding MIs
Newspaper announcements of deaths usually state where burial was to take place so you can find out where to look for a gravestone.

Many burials took place in public cemeteries rather than churchyards. Some cemeteries have existed for centuries; you can use directories (see p. 91) to see what existed in the area, and www.savinggraves.co.uk, which is a county-by-county list of crematoria and cemeteries. Most cemeteries have good records that the staff will search for you, as long as you have a date of death. Graves and memorials to the dead of the two World Wars are well indexed on the Commonwealth War Graves Commission's excellent website www.cwgc.org.

Cremations started at Woking, Surrey, in 1855 but only became popular in the mid-20th century. The Cremation Society of Great Britain can help you work out where your ancestors' ashes may be.

This extraordinary gravestone from the early 19th century, at Delph, Lancashire, is an effective pedigree of the family of William and Jane Whitehead, including a heart-breaking catalogue of their children who died young.

Illegitimacy

In the 19th and 20th centuries roughly 6 per cent of children were born out of wedlock. Sometimes, fathers were named in birth or baptism records, or in associated bastardy bonds in parish chests (see p. 100) and bastardy orders in Quarter Sessions (see p. 103), where they were forced to provide maintenance. Many of these in turn could be reported in local newspapers. In other cases, especially for boys, the father's name would be incorporated into the child's – so Herbert Schofield Langan, illegitimate son of Emma Langan, was almost certainly the son of a Mr Schofield, and probably of a Herbert Schofield, whose existence in the neighbourhood you could confirm through further research. Comparing the DNA (see chapter 10) of the descendant of an illegitimate child with that of a proven descendant of the suspected father can under certain circumstances prove such connections.

Most often, fathers' names were left blank in birth and marriage certificates, and unless the family has stories of who the culprit was, you may never know. Bear in mind that in some cases the mothers themselves wouldn't have known their lover's full name, but before accepting this do look, if possible, at birth *and* baptism records.

A typical bastardy order providing information on a child's paternity.

Institutions

Almshouses run by charities have housed paupers since the Middle Ages. Workhouses have existed since the 17th century and from 1782 they became the main way of caring for the poor and infirm. The system was reorganized in 1834 to create a unified system covering the whole country. The introduction of old age pensions in 1908 and unemployment benefits in 1911 enabled most paupers to remain at home, and the system ended in 1948. The records generally include age, occupation (if any), parish of settlement and why the person needed help. There are also records of births, marriages and deaths of inmates.

Hospitals were founded by the charitable donations of the wealthy or later by the parish, and were often located in the same building as the workhouse.

Local histories

You will learn much useful background on your ancestors' home parishes, and perhaps on your ancestors themselves, from local histories. Antiquarian county histories started being produced properly in the 17th century. Their successors, modern local histories, are still being published today, many by Phillimore. These are best sought via local archives and libraries. The *Victoria County Histories*, which are still being produced, contain much valuable information on the location of enclosure awards, manorial records and locally-useful deeds. See also Stuart Raymond's county bibliographies (see p. 164).

Maps

It's definitely worth seeking historical maps of the places where your ancestors lived, both to get a feel for the area and to see which rivers, canals, roads and railways may have influenced their movements.

Besides county maps showing parish boundaries and ecclesiastical jurisdictions, *The Phillimore Atlas* (see p. 53) also reproduces a series of county maps from 1834. You'll find decorative county maps dating from the 16th century, superceded by ever more accurate ones from the 17th and 18th century. The Ordnance Survey maps of the 19th and 20th centuries are more accurate still but note that some of the copies of old Ordnance Survey maps now for sale, excellent though they are, show late Victorian railways superimposed on maps surveyed some 30 or 40 years earlier. Local archives are the best place to seek relevant historical maps, and a lot is now online at sites such as these:

http://freepages.genealogy.rootsweb. com/~genmaps
Old maps for England, Wales and Scotland, including many links to other map sites.

watch out!
Maps from the 17th and 18th century may show your ancestors' homes, but be aware that mapmakers sometimes drew little pictures of houses as a general rather than an accurate representation of a settlement.

www.yourmapsonline.org.uk
An ever growing collection of out-of-copyright maps submitted by users.

www.genuki.org.uk
This genealogy site has index pages for each county and thus each parish, from which there are links to relevant maps, including some individual parish maps. The gazetteer is at www.genuki.org.uk/big/Gazetteer/.

www.cyndislist/com/maps.htm
Entitled 'Maps, Gazetteers and Geographical Information', this section of the popular genealogy site contains many links to sources for maps.

www.nls.uk/digitallibrary/map
The National Library of Scotland's extensive map collection holds maps of Scotland from 1560 to 1920, including Pont's maps of Scotland dating from about 1583–96 and military maps of Scotland from the 18th century.

www.getamap.ordnancesurvey.co.uk
The Ordnance Survey's website.

Useful too are tithe apportionment maps, made between 1838 and 1854, with copies at county record offices and the National Archives (in series IR 30). Enclosure maps dating from the 17th century were made when shared manorial land was redistributed to create self-contained farms, and deer parks for the owners of the land. Local histories will indicate what is available.

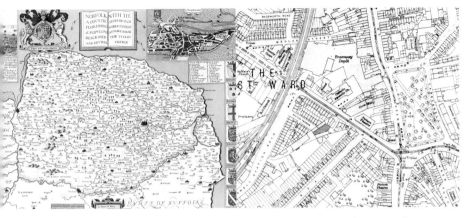

The county of Norfolk, engraved by Jodocus Hondius (1563–1612).

Old Ordnance Survey map from 1913 of Camberwell and Stockwell, London.

Newspapers and magazines

Newspapers started in the 17th century and became widespread on a local level in the 19th. They can contain birth, marriage and death announcements, adverts by tradesmen or professionals, reports of crimes, trials, meetings, burials, and much else that may mention your ancestors. Local papers are best searched in local archives where they are sometimes indexed. The best collection of local, national and foreign papers is at the British Library Newspaper Library whose catalogue is at www.bl.uk/collections/newspapers.html. Announcements concerning the great, good and bad, from military medal recipients to bankrupts, appear in the *London Gazette* (1665 – present); *Gentleman's Magazine* (1731–1868) and *The Times* (1785 [as *The Daily Universal Register*] – present), indexed in *The Times* Digital Archive, all of which can be searched in person or via a record agent at the Guildhall Library, London. Scotland's extensive newspaper output can be examined at the

National Library of Scotland, and *The Scotsman*
(1817 - present) is now fully online up to 1900 at
www.archive.scotsman.com.

Newspaper reports for the death
of my great-grandmother in a car
accident, and the funeral of her
husband's cousin Walter Nursey.

.U. THUNSDAY, MAI

One dead, 6 hurt in West accident

Two Falmouth people were among seven injured when two cars collided at Windwhistle, near Chard on Thursday. One of the injured, 83-year-old Mrs. Winifred Walters, of St. Kilda, Purley-avenue, Purley, Surrey, died in hospital at Taunton yesterday.

Travelling in the same car as Mrs. Walters were Desmond Jago (22), of 8, Claremont-terrace, Falmouth, who received chest injuries; Eileen Shield (27), of 152, Hiltingbury-road, Chandlers Ford, Southampton, who received a fractured pelvis and nose; and Miss Anne Young (23), of 13, Cliff-road, Falmouth, who received lacerations.

The occupants of the other car were Bertram Blonn (45) who had a severely cut tongue; Keith Blonn (10), who had a fractured skull, and Garry Blonn (19), who received shock and bruising, all of 10, Ivel-way, Crewkerne.

All except Miss Young and Garry Blonn were detained in hospital. *w/ m al an 15/4/61*

FUNERAL OF W. R. NURSEY

MANY PAID TRIBUTE

Numerous Telegrams and Floral Gifts—Veterans of '66, St. George's Society and Argonauts Present.

Attended by many former friends, funeral of late Walter Robt. Nursey, writer, soldier, judiciary and wanderer, took place from apartment of Miss Mabel Tibaudeau, Maitland Apartments to St. James' Cemetery.

Miss Thibaudeau, daughter of an old friend of the deceased, had nursed him through his last illness. Service was conducted by Rev. Canon Hilliard of Dixon, chaplain to Veterans of '66 association, and was very simple, following Church of England ritual. The casket was literally covered with floral tributes, many of them from friends of the deceased, living in all parts of Canada and the U.S., and two specially large wreaths were laid on from the Veterans of '66 Association and the St. George's Society.

Since Monday morning telegrams and letters of condolence have been pouring into the apartment from friends all over the country, two of them being from Hon. Jacques Bureau and Judge Hardy. The honorary pall bearers were chosen from the Veterans of '66 Association, and members of St. George's Society also acted as active pall-bearers. They were J. C. Hetherington, Harland

Parish chest material

This term is given to the documentation generated
by the parish, from churchwardens' accounts to
rate books, aside from the parish registers themselves. It is so called because it was kept inside an
iron-bound chest. Most is now in county record
offices, the catalogues of which are at
www.a2a.org.uk.

The equivalent in Scotland are the 'Kirk Sessions',
whose records are largely deposited at the National
Archives of Scotland. Towns tended to have their
own borough records, usually in municipal archives,
that shed much light on their inhabitants, in
particular the poor and the burgesses.

Prisoners

The fate of most criminals was branding and flogging, execution or transportation. Public execution, usually by hanging, was a commonplace event and a cheap form of entertainment in the days before television, often generating souvenir pamphlets and prints. It was abolished in 1868, by which time the death penalty was rarely applied to offences other than murder.

In the Middle Ages, prisons were generally used for those awaiting trial. It was only in the 16th century that Houses of Correction started to be built to hold criminals (and other wrongdoers, like vagrants and pregnant single women) for punishment. With so many hanged or transported for the most minor thieving offenses, however, prisons of the sort we know today did not really come into being until the 19th century. From 1823, records of prisons appear in Quarter Session court reports (see p. 103), which can be found in county record offices, along with gaolers' journals that usually provide names and dates of admission and discharge, and details of the offence.

The National Archives has 'criminal registers' in series HO 26-7, arranged annually from 1805 to 1892, with names, date and place of trial and details of the verdict and punishment. These are partially indexed on Stuart Tamblin's *Criminal Register Index* 1805–40 (CD-ROM), available from www.fhindexes.co.uk. Those for London and Middlesex go back to 1791. Different 'calendars of prisoners' date back in some cases to 1774 in the National Archives (in HO 8, HO 23, HO 24 and PCOM 2, ADM 6, HO 9, HO 7, KB 32, T 38, T 1 and WO 25). Many county record offices have 'prison registers', which usually provide birthplace, age and a physical description and perhaps even a photograph. Scottish prisoners' records are at the National Archives of Scotland: few survive before the mid-19th century.

The hanging of John Thurtell at Hertford Jail in 1824.

Quarter Sessions

These were local courts dealing with a vast amount of business – criminal and civil – that, indirectly or not, touched the lives of most of our ancestors. They are a fabulous resource for family history.

Quarter Sessions were held in each county four times a year from 1361 to 1971. Presided over by Justices of the Peace (JPs) or Magistrates drawn (usually) from the local nobility or gentry, they dealt with minor crimes, such as theft and poaching, and handled many local government matters, such as licensing innkeepers, gamekeepers and itinerant traders; prosecuting Catholics; enforcing the poor law; local militias; maintenance of roads and bridges; and overseeing matters relating to apprenticeship, qualification of craftsmen and tax collection. The records comprise rolls (later books) of 'orders' detailing decisions made by the JPs; 'minutes' or

must know

Originals only
The only drawback of Quarter Session court records is that they are seldom transcribed or indexed, but if you have an idea of when an ancestor may have appeared, or just have some spare time in the archive, they are well worth a search.

'processes' recording the sittings; and 'indictments' detailing criminal charges, with some information about the accused and victims, and much enrolled evidence. There were also records made by others that had to be enrolled with the Quarter Sessions, such as sworn statements; lists of prisoners, jurors, voters, freemasons and householders liable for paying county rates; details of people born abroad (from 1792); bonds and sureties; tax returns; enclosure awards; and much other paraphernalia concerning the contemporary lives of our ancestors.

The records are held at county record offices and detailed in J. Gibson's *Quarter Sessions Records for Family Historians: A Select List* (FFHS, 4th edn, 1995), which also notes the relatively little that has been published. Those for Scotland are at the National Archives of Scotland.

Settlement records

From 1601, anyone who had lived in a parish for a month was entitled to claim poor relief. This money came straight out of the pockets of the other inhabitants, and impecunious newcomers were not generally welcomed. The 1662 Settlement Act limited the right to claim poor relief to the following incomers:

- Wives of men settled in the parish; office holders and rate payers.
- Those renting property in the parish worth over £10.
- Unmarried people who had worked in the parish for over a year.

- Legitimate children under seven whose fathers were settled in the parish.
- Illegitimate children who were born in the parish (until 1744).
- Apprentices whose masters lived in the parish.
- Anyone who had stayed in the parish over 40 days having previously informed the parish that they were going to do so.

Settlement examination of Ann Nursey, single woman, in 1767. Ann states here that she was born in Fressingfield, Norfolk, but later moved with her parents to Stradbrooke.

must know
Recording the poor
Settlement records, linking people from their place of residence to their place of origin, are among the most useful of their kind of local record for genealogists, not least because they record the movements of the otherwise over-looked poor.

The vestry or Justices of the Peace conducted 'settlement examinations' to determine whether newcomers were settled legally and the records provide marvellous details of incomers' places of birth and family circumstances. If people had no right of settlement a 'removal order', issued by a Justice of the Peace, could be used to repatriate them to their parish of settlement (from 1795 this only happened to people actually in need of relief and not too sick to travel). After 1834, paupers were sent to the workhouse covering their place of settlement.

From 1697, to be able to settle elsewhere without this molestation, people obtained 'settlement certificates' from their parish of settlement. By handing these in to the vestry of the parish where they wanted to live, they indemnified it from having to support them if they fell on hard times. Few settlement certificates were kept or have survived for the great towns and cities of the Industrial Revolution, but many have survived for the countryside. They are best sought through the county record office, where some are well indexed.

Taxes

Land Tax was levied from 1693 to 1963, but most records survive between 1780 and 1832. Arranged by parish they list all land-holders with property worth 20 shillings or more and (from 1772) tenants. Window Tax, a replacement for Hearth Tax (see p. 64), was a tax on the number of windows in houses, raised from 1696 until 1851. Paupers were exempt, but not many paupers' cottages had windows anyway. Most surviving records are in county record offices and outlined in *Land and*

Window Tax Assessments by J. Gibson, M. Medlycott and D. Mills (FFHS, 1998).

There were many amusing Georgian taxes, such as tax on male servants (1777–1852), hair powder (1795–1861) and dogs (1796–1882) – records for these and many more are to be found in county record offices and the National Archives.

want to know more?

Further reading and records:
• Deeds: N.W. Alcock's *Old Title Deeds: A Guide for Local and Family Historians* (Phillimore, 1986) and my *Tracing your Home's History* (Collins, 2006) provide help in reading and understanding these complex documents.
• Court cases: Much detail on courts is given in D.T. Hawkings' *Criminal Ancestors: A Guide to Historical Criminal Records in England & Wales* (Sutton, 1992) and M. Herber's *Ancestral Trails* (Sutton Publishing & SoG, 1997, repr. 2000).
• Cremations: See my article on the extraordinary history of cremation, 'Ashes to ashes', in *Family History Monthly*, March 2003.
• Criminal records: A detailed guide to all aspects of criminal records is D.T. Hawkings' *Criminal Ancestors: A Guide to Historical Criminal Records in England & Wales* (Sutton, 1992).
• Institutions: Records are mainly held locally – see www.workhouses.org.uk. Many workhouses and similar institutions are covered on www.institutions.org.uk.
• Weird taxes: See my article 'Hired Hands, Hounds, Hair and Horses: Unusual Georgian Taxes' in *Family History Monthly*, March 2006, no. 128.

6 What people did

Whatever your ancestors did, it's worth finding out what records their occupations may have generated. These can be used to expand your family history. They sometimes give ages, places of birth or fathers' names, so can often help to overcome problems encountered in tracing family origins too.

Occupations

Occupations were often passed down in families and marriages were regularly of 'like to like', creating fascinating networks of interrelated tradesmen or professional families. Women tended to work as hard as men, but their occupations were often menial or concealed behind the work of their husbands.

Schools

Records of educational establishments, from admission registers to school magazines, can add much interesting detail to family histories. Their registers often detail the student's age and father's name and residence so are useful for genealogy too.

Many very good schools for the poor (usually up to age 13) existed from the 17th century. Mass education only began with the Education Act of 1870 (1872 in Scotland), but schools often charged small fees, thus putting the poor off, even after an act of 1880 made attendance for all under 10s and most under 13s compulsory. Free secondary education for children up to 18 started in some places from 1880 but was not generally available until after 1902.

Fish Fags by Thomas Rowlandson (1756–1827). Many women's occupations in the past tended to be decidedly unglamorous.

Many schools still have their own records, and those of many others have been deposited in local archives. Admission registers of fee-paying schools (i.e. private and public schools, the latter being the cream of the fee-paying sector) are often published and accessible in libraries, with a good collection at the Society of Genealogists. You'll often find more than one member of the family and sometimes several generations in the same school records.

Claude Lorraine Richard Wilson Nursey (1816–73), headmaster of Belfast School of Design.

A Stonyhurst speech day programme from 1833, including my cousin Richard Havers.

Prologue, ...	RICHARD CORR
Two Books of Livy—Agricola of Tacitus—De Amicitia and seven Orations of Cicero—two Orations of Isocrates—one Book of Thucydides—and two Books of Herodotus.	RICHARD COOPER / FRANCIS AYLWARD / RICHARD AYLWARD / CHRISTOPHER GALLWEY / JOSEPH HARTING / RICHARD HAVERS
Extract from a Speech of Lord Chatham against the adoption of coercive measures in America. . . .	CHRISTOPHER GALLWEY
The same translated into Latin prose.	EDWARD BARON
Extract from a Speech of Mr. Canning, on a motion respecting peace with the French Republick.	
The same translated into Greek prose. . . .	JOSEPH HARTING / AMADEE VILAIN XIIII.
On Magnanimity.	JOHN RAPHAEL
The Aeneid (the fourth Book excepted)—and twelve Books of the Iliad.	JOSEPH NIND / PATRICK BREEN / JOHN PILKINGTON / ALEXANDER KNIGHT / GREGORY DOYLE / ADOLPHUS GILLET / EDWARD WRIGHT / JOSEPH BOND / THOMAS SEGRAVE
Extract from Paradise Lost, Book 1st. . . .	JOSEPH BOND
The same translated into Greek Hexameter Verse. . .	ALEXANDER KNIGHT
Extract from the Pleasures of Hope. Campbell. . .	GABRIEL VRIGNON
The same translated into Latin Elegiack Verse. . .	RICHARD NORRIS
Death of the Duke D'Enghien—an Elegy. . . .	PATRICK BREEN
Montezuma—Carmen, ...	JOHN PILKINGTON
Herod Agrippa—a Poem.	ADOLPHUS GILLET

Universities

Oxford and Cambridge were the only two universities in England and Wales before the establishment of Durham in 1832. Their registers have been published, with varying degrees of biographical information added:

• A.B. Emden, *A Biographical Register of the University of Cambridge to 1500* (CUP, 1963).

• J. and J.A.Venn, *Alumni Cantabrigiensi: A Biographical List of All Known Students, Graduates and Holders of Office at the University of Cambridge from the Earliest Times to 1900* (CUP, 1922–7 and 1940–54).

• A.B. Emden, *A Biographical Register of the University of Oxford to AD 1500* (OUP, 1957) and another volume *1501–40* (OUP, 1974).

• J. Foster, *Alumni Oxoniensis: The Members of the University of Oxford 1500–1714; their Parentage, Birthplace and Year of Birth, with a Record of their Degrees...* (James Parker & Co., 1891)

• *Alumni Oxoniensis: The Members of the University of Oxford 1715–1886* (James Parker & Co., 1888–91)

Similar works exist for other universities, especially those founded in the 19th century (Durham, London and so on).

Scotland has four pre-Reformation universities – St Andrew's, Aberdeen, Glasgow and Edinburgh. All are with published lists and excellent archives. Ireland has one – Trinity College, Dublin – whose published registers are: G.D. Burtchaell and T.U. Sadlier (eds), *Alumni Dublinenses: A register of the Students, Graduates, Professors and Provosts of Trinity College, in the University of Dublin* (Williams & Norgate, 1924).

Since the mid-19th century the numbers of universities and people educated in them has increased enormously.

Some British students went abroad, particularly to Leyden or Heidelberg if they were Protestants or Spain, Portugal, France and Italy if Catholics. The Catholic Record Society has published many records of Catholics educated in universities and also of the English Catholic schools established abroad when Catholicism was still illegal here in the 18th century.

Apprentice, master and freeman

Journeymen were unqualified labourers, paid daily – hence their name, from the French for a day (jour). Others who practised a trade received training through the system of apprenticeships.

Many children, mainly boys, were bound to a master, usually for seven years between the ages of 10 and 18, for a fee. Apprentices were then 'freed' and if they submitted a test-piece, called a 'master-piece', which passed muster, they qualified to become a master craftsman. Some towns and cities such as London have good records of apprenticeships contracted there. Many apprenticeships between 1710 and 1774 were taxed by the Inland Revenue and records of them are indexed at the Society of Genealogists and on the Origins Network http://www.originsnetwork.com/help/aboutbo-appgb2.htm. They almost always provide fathers' names and places of residence, so are a great way of linking back from a tradesman in one place to his roots elsewhere.

Many towns and cities were corporations, with rights to trade and vote restricted to freemen. You could usually become a freeman either by apprenticeship, honour (having it bestowed on you), patrimony (being the son of a freeman) or redemption (buying your way in). Some corporations had an intermediary grade of guild membership, which then subsequently qualified one to become a freeman. Records are usually in municipal archives and many have been published.

The record of my grandfather's grant of freedom in 1933, making him a Freeman of the City of London.

The foregoing system applied especially in London, where all guilds (except those of the watermen, lightermen and parish clerks) were called 'livery companies' because of the bright costumes or 'liveries' that the Crown allowed them to parade about in. The records are mostly at Guildhall Library; many have published histories and much information is now on www.englishorigins.net. Records of London freemen survive from after the Great Fire (1666) and are at the Corporation of London Record Office. Many such urban corporations had their own civil courts. Those for the City of London, for example, included the Court of Hustings and Mayor's Court and go back to the 14th century: they are at the Corporation of London Record Office.

Other sources for occupations

- **Biographical dictionaries:** These generally cover people in the context of what they did. *The Oxford Dictionary of National Biography* (www.oup.com/oxforddnb) contains some 50,000 articles on all manner of Britons, including limited information on their family connections. Many occupations have specialist biographical dictionaries, such as *Britten's Old Clocks and Watches and their Makers* by G.H. Baillie (ed.) (9th edn, 1982) and *The Commissioned Sea Officers of the Royal Navy 1660-1815* by D. Syrett and R.L. DiNardo (Naval Records Society, 1994). *Specialist Indexes for Family Historians* by J. Gibson and E. Hampson (FFHS, 1998) includes many indexes to people in various occupations, from brushmakers to mathematicians.
- **Genealogy magazines:** *Ancestors, Family History Monthly, Family Tree Magazine, Practical Family History* and *Your Family Tree* have run articles on many occupations and their records. See, for example, my article 'Artists' in *Family History Monthly* (April 2003, no. 91). All these magazines are stocked in W.H. Smith and can be ordered through any good newsagent.

must know

Tracing professions
Many professionals attended universities (see p. 111) and specialist professional institutions that recorded ages and fathers' names, making their origins relatively easy to trace, not least because sons often followed fathers into the same profession.

Professionals

Lawyers can be traced from 1775 through published *Law Lists*, and the Law Society has good records. Barristers were lawyers called to practise at the bar through one of the Inns of Court, the main being Lincoln's Inn, Gray's Inn, Middle Temple and Inner Temple, whose admission registers contain useful details. If promoted to become judges they will be in E. Foss's *A Biographical Dictionary of the Judges of England, 1066–1870* (John Murray, 1870).

Clergymen can be traced through the records of their denomination. There are frequently specialist denominational biographical dictionaries for them. Anglican clergymen almost all attended university (see p. 111) and their wills were generally proved in the PCC (Prerogative Court of Canterbury – see p. 68). Early clergy are listed by the Institute of Historical Research at www.british-history.ac.uk and

The Doctor by Arthur Miles (c.1860).

later ones are in the *Clerical Guide* (from 1817), the *Clergy List* (from 1841) and *Crockford's Clerical Directory* (from 1858).

Doctors were traditionally far less educated. From 1511 to 1775, licenses to practise medicine were issued by bishops' courts. They are listed in the *Medical Directory* (from 1845) and the *Medical Register* (from 1859). Excellent secondary sources for many doctors, dentists and midwives include the following: *Eighteenth Century Medics (Subscriptions, Licenses, Apprenticeships)* by P.J. and R.V. Wallis (Project for Historical Geography Research Series, 1994) and *The Medical Practitioners in Medieval England: A Biographical Register* by C.H. Talbot and E.A. Hammond (Wellcome Historical Medical Library, 1965).

My great-great-grandfather, Rev. Patrick Henry Kilduff, a clergyman in Tottenham, London, who trained at Trinity College, Dublin.

Policemen

Sir Robert Peel's 'peace preservation police force' was established in London in the second decade of the 19th century but the Metropolitan Police proper wasn't formed until 1829. Its records up to the 1930s are in National Archives series MEPO, described in information leaflet 53. Subsequent records are at the Metropolitan Police Historical Museum. The Police Orders Metropolitan Police Database is at http://www.policeorders.co.uk.

The earliest county police forces started being formed in 1835 and all counties had one by 1858. Their records are held variously by the constabularies or local record offices, as detailed in L.A. Waters' *Notes for Family Historians* (Police History Society, 1987). The Police Historical Society is at www.policehistorysociety.co.uk.

The Palestine Police kept the peace in Palestine (modern Palestine and Israel) between 1922 and 1948 and included many British members. The best records to start searching are those at the British Empire and Commonwealth Museum. My articles 'Law and Order (the history and records of the Palestine Police)' are in *Practical Family History*, January and February 2006 (nos. 97 and 98).

Businesses

Many businesses were founded by and for families. Their records of appointment of directors and shareholders may therefore reveal names of many relations, male and female, and add a fascinating extra layer to a family history. Equally, many kept records of employees that can be helpful in your research. Existing companies may have good archives. Archives of defunct ones may be in archives (see www.a2a.org.uk) and can also be sought through Companies House and the Business Archives Council.

My great-grandfather Herman Julius Rietchel and a page from his employment records at Sun Life. He later rose to become the firm's general manager. Because the record was made before the First World War, it records him under his original, German spelling, 'Rietschel'.

Clubs and societies

Membership records of clubs and societies contain much that is useful for family history and, sometimes, for tracing origins when stuck. There were many friendly societies, such as the 'Oddfellows', to which our poorer ancestors belonged, paying small subscriptions in return for financial support in times of need. Most records are still with local branches, or local record offices. Trades Unions were established from the mid-19th century. Branch records are the best ones to use, as they may provide details of your ancestor in terms of joining, transfer from one branch to another, payment of benefits such as sick pay, funeral benefits and benefits for widows and orphans. The records can be sought through the union itself or at the relevant county record office. Many are listed in *Trade Union & Related Records* by J. Bennett, A. Tough and R. Storey (University of Warwick, 6th edn, 1991).

must know

Freemasons

Members of all classes could become Freemasons. Their details can be sought via local Freemasonic Lodge records or from the Grand Secretaries of the Freemasons' Halls in London, Edinburgh and Dublin. More details are given in my article 'Squaring the Freemason Circle' in *Ancestors* (December 2004, issue 28).

The services

Many ancestors were in the services before returning home to marry and have children. You'll often find a mention of this, say, in a child's baptism entry, but sometimes you'll only learn about their exciting early lives if you specifically look in the relevant records.

Militia records

Records of ordinary men liable to serve in the county militias from the 16th to the early 20th century are in county record offices, with some in the National Archives, National Library of Wales and National Archives of Scotland. A few are in print. Some 19th-century records include births and baptisms of serving militiamen's children (in National Archives series WO 32 and WO 68). See W. Spencer, *Records of the Militia and Volunteer Forces* (PRO Publications, 1997) and J. Gibson and M. Medlycott, *Militia Lists and Musters 1757–1876: A Directory of Holdings in the British Isles* (FFHS, 3rd edn, 1994).

The army

The main army records are in National Archives department WO (War Office), though much extra information is in dedicated museums.

Officers

Until the 20th century, officers were almost entirely from the middle and upper classes, with ranks down from general, colonel, lieutenant colonel, major, captain, 1st lieutenant and 2nd lieutenant.

Battle of Agincourt, 1415.
An exhausted force of 9,000 soldiers, mainly foot-soldiers and archers, scored a collosal defeat of the French cavalry. Sadly, few non-noble participants' names were ever recorded.

Medieval armies were ad hoc affairs, drawn from the land-holding aristocracy and their tenants. The standing army was first established in 1660 and initially you are only likely to find mention of officers. The period to 1727 is covered by C. Dalton's *English Army Lists and Commission Registers 1661–1714* (Eyre & Spottiswoode, 1892–1904; repr. Francis Edwards, 1960) and *George the First's Army 1714–27* (Eyre & Spottiswoode, 1910–12). From 1740 there have been regular *Army Lists*, listing all officers and giving basic details about them, accessible in the National Archives and the Society of Genealogists.

Regiments

The army was divided into regiments. Most have excellent museums and published histories that provide background information and may have details or pictures of your ancestor. An online guide is www.army.mod.uk.unit sandorgs and enquiries can also be made through the Army Museum Ogilby Trust and Imperial War Museum.

The Victoria Cross awards for the army, 1857.

The National Archives has much documentation on officers, the main being 'services of officers on the active list' in series WO 25 and 76 (partially indexed, dating back to 1829 and in some cases to 1764), including age and place of birth.

Records of First World War officers are indexed at www.catalogue.nationalarchives.gov.uk.

Officers' diaries

Many officers' official diaries are at the National Archives, giving background on the men's activities and occasionally naming some of them. Those for the First World War are becoming available on the site www.documentsonline.nationalarchives.gov.uk.

Medals

Medal rolls, which tell you by implication the campaigns in which men served, are in National Archives series WO 372. Those for the First World War, which partially substitute those service records that are lost, are online at www.documentsonline.nationalarchives.gov.uk. Also contact the Army Medals Office.

Other ranks

Non-officers' service records from 1760 to 1854 are indexed in the National Archives catalogue, through which the records themselves can be sought. Because records are generally arranged by regiment, for soldiers after 1854 it's best to try to discover their regiment from a mention in a census or on the birth record of a child. Besides service records, you can also use muster rolls, pay lists (a few of which go back to 1708), description books (some back to 1754)

18th-century soldiers on parade outside St James's Palace. Note the multi-racial mix even then, with black bandsmen and white soldiers.

and records of casualty, desertion, attestation, discharge, prisoners of war and pensions. Pensions were paid through Chelsea, and through Kilmainham (Dublin) for all soldiers demobbed in Ireland, and these can also be a short-cut to learning a soldier's regiment after 1854.

War deaths

First and Second World War armed forces deaths are indexed at www.1837online.com and the Family Records Centre. Deaths, war graves and war memorials are indexed by the Commonwealth War Graves Commission at www.cwgc.org.

First World War memorial.

must know
First World War
Many other ranks' service papers were blown up, but some 2 million are still extant, so it's always worth searching for an ancestor here. The many published memorials include the *National Roll of the Great War 1914–1918* (National Publishing Company, 1918–21), containing information on about 150,000 men, alive or dead.

Home Guard

Records of the real life 'Dad's Army', the Home Guard, are in National Archives series WO 199, 166 and PREM 3.

The Royal Marines

Established in 1665 to serve as soldiers on navy ships, the Royal Marines fall into three divisions: Chatham, Plymouth and Portsmouth. Records are in department ADM (Admiralty) at the National Archives, in whose Research Enquiries Room is (in particular) a card index to most attestation forms (ADM 157/1–659).

'Captain, Flag Officer and Commander' from *Costume of the Royal Navy and Marines*, engraved by L. and E. Mansion (19th century).

The Royal Navy

The Royal Navy was created by Henry VIII in 1546 with records (mainly for the 18th century onwards) at the National Archives in department ADM (Admiralty).

Officers

There were commissioned officers (admiral, rear admiral, commodore, commander, captain and lieutenant) and warrant officers, who were in charge of functional aspects of the ship such as master, engineer, sailmaker, gunner, boatswain, surgeon and carpenter. Commissioned officers between 1660 to 1845 are outlined in the following books:

- J. Charnock's *Biographia Navalis, Or Impartial Memoirs of the Lives and Characters of Officers of the Navy of Great Britain* (R. Faulder, 1794–8).
- J. Marshall's *Royal Naval Biography* (Longman, Hurst, Rees, Orme & Brown, 1823–35).
- W.R. O'Byrne's *A Naval Biographical Dictionary* (John Murray, 1849, repr. 1861).
- *Navy Lists*, which were published from 1782.
- *The Naval Who's Who 1917* covers many First World War officers.

Officers' service papers and other records are at the National Archives.

Ratings

Until 1853, non-officers (also known as 'ratings') were only employed – sometimes even against their will – per voyage, so can be very hard to locate in ships' musters: if you can't guess the ship, you may not find them. From 1853 to 1923 ratings appear in 'continuous service engagement books', fully indexed in National Archives records ADM 188/245–267, which give dates and places of birth.

must know
Dockyards
The main Royal Navy dockyards were Portsmouth, Woolwich, Deptford, Chatham, Sheerness and Plymouth, and many naval families moved between them. The main British ones abroad were Halifax in Nova Scotia, Port Royal in Jamaica, and Gibraltar. National Archives department ADM contains records of dockyard clerks or tradesmen from the 1660s, and the National Maritime Museum has a detailed card index to these people.

Muster rolls in ADM 36–39 (1740–1808, with a few back to 1688) can lead you from ship to ship, and will tell you ages and places of birth from 1764, together with other details such as tobacco and clothing allowances. Pay books, seamen's effects papers, medal rolls, description books and pension records can also be consulted at the National Archives. Pensions were paid through the Chatham Chest (records exist from 1653–7 and 1675–1799) and later from the Royal Naval Hospital, Greenwich.

A continuous service agreement.

The Merchant Navy

The 'Merchant Navy' is the term given to all the British ships not in the Royal Navy. Their records are in National Archives department BT (Board of Trade). There are some muster rolls from 1747, but most are from the mid-19th century. Records are generally arranged by port, making them very hard to search except between 1835 and 1857, which are indexed in the 'registers of seamen' (BT 120, 112, 119 and 114), which lead straight to crew lists (BT 98), which in turn give age and place of birth. BT 114 can also be used to look up 'seamens' tickets' (1845–53), which include date and place of birth. After 1857, searching reverts to being very hard, until 1913–41, which is covered by a Central Index Register of Seamen at the National Archives.

Much British merchant naval material, including many post-1861 crew lists, is now at the Maritime History Archive (Newfoundland), which offers an online search service. Those who died at sea

Merchant Ships under Sail and at Anchor off a Town by William Anderson (1757–1837).

must know

Pensions

Trinity House, London, issued pensions to retired seamen or their widows and orphans between 1514 and 1854. A.J. Camp's *The Trinity House Petitions: A Calendar of the Records of the Corporation of Trinity House, London* (SoG, 1987) details applications made to the Trinity House charity from 1787 to 1854 by needy ex-sailors and their families from both the Royal and Merchant Navies.

between 1852 and 1889 are indexed in BT 154. Further records that you can search include ships' log books. Many boys and men were trained for the Merchant Navy by the Marine Society, whose indexed registers 1772–1950 are at the National Maritime Museum. Medals awarded to merchant seamen who served in the Second World War – some 100,000 of them – are now searchable online at www.documentsonline.nationalarchives.gov.uk.

Merchant Navy captains were called 'master mariners', and second-in-commands were 'mates'. From 1845 (and compulsorily from 1850), new masters and mates could obtain a 'certificate of competency'. Including year and place of birth, the records are indexed in BT 127. Other records of them include a list covering 1868 to 1947, stating date and place of birth, in Lloyd's Marine Collection at the Guildhall Library, London.

The Royal Air Force

The Royal Air Force (RAF) was formed in 1918 by amalgamating the army's Royal Flying Corps and the navy's Royal Naval Air Service, founded in 1912 and 1914 respectively, whose main records are in National Archives (NA) series WO 363, 364 and ADM 273 respectively. Women's RAF records for the First World War are at the NA in AIR 80. Post 1918, records are in department AIR accompanied by published *Air Force Lists*. See W. Spencer, *Air Force Records for Family Historians* (PRO, 2002) and the RAF Museum for more information.

RAF flyers in England during the Second World War.

Recent records

Armed forces records less than 80 years old are only released to next-of-kin. If you can prove you are the next-of-kin of a deceased serviceman you can apply to the relevant agency: Army Records Centre, Royal Marines Historical Records and Medals, RAF Personnel and Training Command or Royal Naval Personnel Records Office.

want to know more?

Further reading:
- Schools: Excellent background information is in C.R. Chapman's *The Growth of British Education and its Records* (Lochin Publishing, 2nd edn, 1992).
- Town records: The best account of municipal records, including much to do with freemen, is J. West's *Town Records* (Phillimore, 1983).
- Old occupations: R. Campbell's *The London Tradesman* (1747, reprinted 1969 by David & Charles) is a great way of finding out what many old occupations actually entailed – wherever your ancestors lived. Useful too is S.A. Raymond's *Londoners' Occupations: A Genealogical Guide* (FFHS, 1994) and D.R. Torrance's *Scottish Trades and Professions: A Selected Bibliography* (SAFHS, 1991).
- Army: Useful guides include S. Fowler's *Army Records for Family Historians* (PRO Publications, 2nd edn, 1998, revised by W. Spencer), M.J. and C. Watts's, *My Ancestor was in the British Army: How can I find out more about him?* (SoG, repr. 1995), S. Fowler's *Tracing your First World War Ancestor* (Countryside Books, 2003) and S. Fowler's *Tracing your Second World War Ancestor* (Countryside Books, 2005).
- Royal Marines: Read G. Thomas's *Records of Royal Marines* (PRO Publications, 1994). Also useful is the Royal Marines Museum.
- Royal Navy: Read B. Pappalardo's *Tracing Your Naval Ancestors* (TNA, 2003) and N.A.M. Rodger's *Naval Records for Genealogists* (PRO Publications, 3rd edn, 1998), and visit the National Maritime Museum and Royal Naval Museum.
- Merchant Navy: Read *My Ancestor was a Merchant Seaman* by C. and M. Watts (3rd edition, SoG, 2004).

7 Immigration and emigration

Since the original pre-Bronze Age people of the British Isles, there have been countless immigrations adding to the rich soup of the British gene-pool. The comings and goings of people between the British Isles and the rest of the world are a feature of all our family trees, and have generated some of the most interesting records.

Incomers

We all have ancestors who were born outside Britain. Tracing back to the original immigrant is usually reasonably straightforward, but then the big question arises: 'Where did that person come from?' Fortunately, British bureaucracy generated a great series of records – a godsend to researchers.

First inhabitants

Although Britain has been inhabited by humans on and off for the past 680,000 years, our present occupation started towards the end of the Upper Paleolithic, some 10,000 years ago, when the Ice Age ended and bands of people – the Cro-Magnon cave-dwellers of southern Europe – followed herds of mammoth and bison into these lands. By 8,400 years ago, the rising sea (caused by the melting of ice) cut the British Isles off from Europe, leaving barely 2,000 people stranded here. DNA technology shows that their genes still form the core of the modern population.

These original 'British' people are ancestors of anyone with any British ancestry through countless lines of our family tree. You can see their remains at archaeological sites and in museums. Finds at Star Carr near Seamer, Yorkshire, date back some 9,500 years and include sets of antlers whose bases are bored with holes, quite possibly so they could be attached to people's heads for shamanistic dances. The Morris Dancers of Abbotts Bromley, Staffordshire, still perform such a 'horn dance'. By doing so, it's possible they are continuing a tradition that goes back quite literally to our roots in these isles. Sadly, we've absolutely no idea of these ancestors' names or pedigrees.

Many waves of new immigrants have come since, introducing farming techniques and causing great changes to our culture, language and religion. They did not have as great an effect on our gene pool as was thought in the past, however, when it was assumed, for example, that the Saxon incomers of the 5th and 6th centuries AD had entirely displaced the earlier inhabitants of England. Yet all these waves have contributed to our family trees, giving each one of us roots and ancestors from further afield.

Following the Saxons came Vikings, Normans, and many Flemish weavers in the Middle Ages, all of whom contributed to our gene pool and affected the development of the English language.

Gypsies

From at least the 16th century, Gypsies (nomadic peoples descended originally from lower caste Indians) travelled through Britain, slowly Anglicizing their surnames to include Lee, Boswell, Faws and Hern.

Walloons and Huguenots

From the Reformation in the 16th century, a steady wave of Flemish and French Protestants, called 'Walloons' and 'Huguenots' respectively, came here seeking refuge from persecution by the Catholic powers. The years 1572 (the St Bartholemew's Day Massacre) and 1685 (the Revocation of the Edict of Nantes) mark key events in France that caused the greatest waves of migrants. Many settled in specific areas, such as Canterbury, Southampton, Norwich, Bristol and London (especially Spitalfields and Bethnal Green) and engaged in certain trades, such as paper-making and silk weaving. They kept their own records –

must know

Gypsy sources
For tracing and understanding Gypsy ancestry, read S. Floate's *My Ancestors were Gypsies* (SoG, 1999) and join the Romany and Traveller Family History Society.

must know
Huguenot sources
Indispensable guides
for tracing and
understanding
Huguenot ancestry are
Huguenot Ancestry by
Noel Currer-Briggs and
Royston Gambier
(Phillimore, 1985) and
the publications of the
Huguenot Society.

the earliest date from 1567, in Southampton – and
some Huguenot institutions, such as the Huguenot
Chapel in Canterbury Cathedral and La Providence
hospital in Rochester, maintain their unique identity.
But generally they assimilated quickly into the Anglican
population, translating many surnames (Du Pont into
Bridge) or Anglicizing them (Mercier became Mercer).

Other Europeans

Wars in central Europe brought a trickle of
Hungarians, fleeing the Turkish attacks on their
native land in the 17th century. Catholic attacks on
the Protestant Rhone Palatine (in modern Bavaria)
brought some 10,000 'Palatines' fleeing here in
1709, many of whom went on to Ireland (see
www.irishpalatines.org).

Map of East Prussia, 1645.
Many migrants, gentile and
Jews alike, came from here.

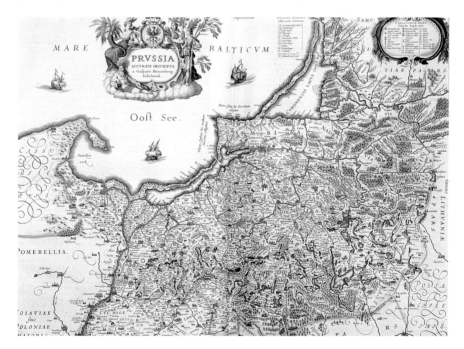

Jews have settled here quietly since the Middle Ages,
and have been welcomed officially since 1655. The
first wave were Sephardic Jews. They were mainly
rich, educated merchants from Venice, Spain and
Portugal, many of whom had sojourned in Holland
prior to coming here. They had names such as
Montefiore, Da Costa and Levy – the surname of the
ancestors of Princess Anne's husband, Commander
Timothy Lawrence, whose family changed their
surname, as so many did, to try to fit in.

The second wave, arriving mainly from the late 18th
century in response to persecution at home, were
Ashkenazi Jews from Germany and eastern Europe.
They were generally peddlers and tradesmen, with
surnames such as Herschel (often Anglicized to Hart)
and Misel, such as the ancestors of actor Warren
Mitchell, who portrayed the xenophobic Alf Garnet in
Till Death Us Do Part, whose ancestors altered their
surname for the same reason. Some Jewish births

Ruby Wax's Jewish ancestry can
be traced to the Wachs family in
eastern Europe.

and burials were registered in Anglican parish registers (though they were exempt from having to marry in Anglican churches) and all are in General Registration. You can also trace Jewish ancestors through synagogue records of birth, *brit milah* (circumcision – for boys), *kethubot* (marriage contracts) and deaths. Such events for well-off Jews were often announced in *The Times*.

Many Germans arrived in the 19th century, including Protestant sugar bakers, and my own ancestor Wilhelm Adolph, a Catholic indigo merchant from Hachenberg in the Grand Duchy of Nassau, whose certificate of arrival in London is dated 6 June 1832.

In the 21st century substantial immigration from eastern Europe has contributed yet more diversity to the British gene pool.

Certificate of Arrival from 1843.

Non-European ancestry

Black people started being brought to Britain as servants (though they were effectively slaves) since the 16th century and were here in considerable numbers by the 18th century. This makes it likely that many 'white' people have at least one black

ancestor. Some had Classical forenames like Caesar
and Pompey, bestowed on them by fanciful masters,
but most were given run-of-the-mill British ones
(like John White or Jack Black). Unless described as
'negro' or 'a black' in parish registers, which does
happen sometimes, the only hint you'll have of a
black ancestor is when you can't trace their origins
here. If the black ancestor was a direct male-line
male ancestor or a direct female-line female one,
DNA tests (see p. 180) can reveal the truth.

More recently, waves of Chinese, Indian, Pakistani
and Commonwealth Caribbean migrants have
enriched our gene pool further, and in the 21st
century substantial immigration from Africa has
contributed to yet more diversity.

Use contact websites to track relatives

In the 22nd century, the average British person will have recent ancestry from all over
the world, including many countries where records are kept poorly, if at all. It is therefore
essential that all families of recent arrival be encouraged to record their pedigrees both
privately and also using contact websites. My view is that www.genesreunited.com is
the ideal vehicle for this and, if enough people take up this suggestion, it will soon
become a formidable resource for future generations.

Needless to say, the British have settled all over the world, not least in the Americas,
Southern Africa, India and the Antipodes. The internet has again proved a remarkably
useful tool for reconnecting branches of families who have lost contact due to great
distances, and DNA can provide proof of connections when records do not.

Tracing ancestry from abroad

Anyone living in Britain but born abroad was an
'alien' and lacked rights, such as the bequeathing of
property. Many put up with this: their British-born
children became British automatically in any case.

British subjects

Denization made the person a British subject by a grant from the Crown, while naturalization made someone a British subject, not just from the date of the grant, but retrospectively – for their entire lives. Until the 19th century naturalization required the taking of Anglican communion, making denization preferable to Jews and Catholics.

Others would seek 'denization' by a crown grant or 'naturalization' by Act of Parliament or, from 1844, by a certificate from the Home Secretary.

Records from 1509 to 1800

The following have been published by the Huguenot Society of London:

- vol 8, W. Page (ed.), *Letters of Denization and Acts of Naturalization for Aliens in England, 1509-1603* (1893).
- vol. 18, W.A. Shaw (ed.), *Letters of Denization and Acts of Naturalization in England and Ireland, 1603-1700* (1911).
- vol. 27, W.A. Shaw (ed.), *Letters of Denization and Acts of Naturalization in England and Ireland, 1701-1800* (1923).

These records usually state places of origin and identify people who came – as they so often did – in groups. From the 19th century onwards you can expect much more in terms of dates of birth, details of spouse and children, residence, occupation, how long they had lived in Britain and why they had migrated.

Records from 1801

Denizations from 1801 to 1900, Parliamentary naturalizations 1801-1947 (whose original records are at the House of Lords Record Office) and Home Secretary's certificates 1844-71 (HO 334) are all indexed in HO 1 at the National Archives and Family Records Centre, while all Home Secretary's certificates are indexed in HO 409/vols 1-11, 1800-1980, though from 1962 the indexes are annual. Correspondence relating to naturalizations and denizations are in HO 1 (1789–1871), HO 45 (1841–78) and HO 144 (1879–1919). The periods 1844–71 (from HO 1), 1872–8 (HO 45) and 1879–1934 (HO 144) are indexed in the NA catalogue at www.catalogue.nationalarchives.gov.uk. Thereafter, 1934–48 can be searched by surname in Ho 405: surnames for that period, from O to Z, are being released in 2007. Files dating from the last 80 years are closed, but you can ask to inspect them under the Freedom of Information Act by pressing the 'Request review' button in the catalogue.

Two naturalization documents, for David Kahn, alias Carr, from Latvia in 1929, and Leonard Reibald from Hesse Darmstadt in 1824.

Other records of aliens

From 1792 all immigrants had to register with a Justice of the Peace, giving name, rank, occupation and address. HO 1 contains a collection of passes granted to aliens between 1793 and 1836, detailing name, nationality, religion and occupation. From 1836 there are certificates noting the arrival of aliens and their place of origin. These are in HO 2, indexed up to 1849 in HO 5/25-32 with related correspondence, 1794-1909, in HO 5. After the First World War, county police forces (see p. 118) kept records of aliens, often including photographs. These are held by the county police archive or the county record office.

Shipping lists

Ships' passenger lists for immigrants from outside Europe are at the National Archives in BT 26, 1878-1960, but as they are arranged chronologically by port of arrival they are highly impractical to search, and they don't state places of origin. HO 3 contains some ships' lists of alien arrivals between 1836 and 1869, indexed 1853-69 by Len Metzner.

Enemy aliens

In the First and Second World Wars, enemy aliens who did not return home were interned in special camps. There is partial coverage of internees in National Archives series WO 900/45-6 (First World War) and HO 214/5 (Second World War) and an index created by the Anglo-German Family History Society. Some, such as doctors, were exempted through 'alien registration certificates', many of which are at the Midlands Police Museum, Birmingham.

Guidelines for tracing origins

Here are some points to bear in mind when seeking immigrant ancestors:

Heinrich Julius Rietschel, an immigrant Saxon lamp salesman, whose sudden death in 1913 saved him from the ignominy of being interned as an enemy alien in the First World War.

- Places of origin are stated more or less accurately in census returns.
- Post-1837, look for the migrant marrying after arrival: the certificate will give you the name and occupation of the father back home.
- From the late 19th century onwards, if immigrants gave their house an unusual name this is likely to be that of their place of origin.
- Wills of migrants may include bequests to relatives, such as siblings, nieces or nephews, in the country of origin.
- Don't forget that countries of origin may have changed their borders. In the 19th century, for example, 'Russia' included much of eastern Europe, including Poland.
- When people gave a place of origin, this might actually have been the nearest town to the obscure village where they'd actually resided.
- Localize the surname using telephone directories, www.familysearch.org (which may actually list your ancestor's foreign baptism) and internet search engines. These will help you establish in which country, and where within that country, the surname was most common. You can then seek your ancestor's birth there.
- Occupations provide clues sometimes. A 19th century tailor in an industrial town could well have been a Jew from eastern Europe, for example, and a silk dyer in London, Norwich, Southampton or Canterbury would probably have had Huguenot ancestry.

Emigrants

Many people migrated from Britain, mainly to inhabit new colonies, either voluntarily as settlers or involuntarily as convicts. Generally, emigration from Britain was poorly recorded, though many countries of arrival kept records of incomers.

must know

www.cyndislist.com
This is unquestionably the most useful resource for archives, researchers, societies and contacts all over the world.

Irish ancestry

Many Irish immigrants flooded into America due to the Potato Famine of 1845-7. Those who couldn't afford the journey came to mainland Britain, mainly settling in London and the industrial cities of the north, particularly Liverpool. Often you'll find ancestors in censuses stating they were born in Ireland but not specifying where, or just stating the county, not the parish. As Irish General Registration only started in 1864, this can pose enormous problems. With luck, though, you'll find a mainland General Registration marriage certificate, stating the father's name, thus giving you a name to look up in two reasonably comprehensive lists, the Tithe Applotment Books and Primary Griffith's Valuation.

Tithe records date from 1823 to 1837 and list, parish by parish, the occupiers of all agricultural land, the name of the land, the landlord and the amount of tithes deemed to be payable. 'Griffith's Valuation', as it is usually known, dates from 1847 to 1865 and records the landlords and occupiers of all buildings and land, noting the nature of the holding, with precise size and rateable value, within each poor law union. Both records are at the National Archives in Dublin, with copies in libraries such as that of the Society of Genealogists, and are

searchable at www.irishorigins.com and
http://scripts.ireland.com/ancestor/ (both of which
include many more useful resources for Irish
ancestry). Having found possible entries, you can
search the surviving registers of the relevant parishes
for the baptism of the migrant ancestor.

Sadly, Ireland's troubled history is reflected in its
parish registers. Most of its roughly 1,600
(Protestant) Church of Ireland parish registers were
blown up by the IRA. What survives is with the
Representative Church Body Library in Dublin with
copies on microfiche at the Public Record Office of

Migrants to America. In the Land of Promise by Charles Frederic Ulrich (1858-1908).

Northern Ireland. Most people, however, were Catholics. Due to poverty and Catholicism being technically illegal until the 1820s, few registers were kept before then – but there is much thereafter. The registers are mostly still in the parishes but you'll find some at county Heritage Centres, for which see www.scripts.ireland.com/ancestor/browse/addresses/major.htm, with microfiche copies of many at the National Library of Ireland.

Transportees

Large numbers of criminals were transported to British colonies. Many of the early settlers in America and the Caribbean were transportees and, once the American War of Independence put pay to this, prisoners were sent, from 1788, to Australia instead. The main sources for pre-Australian

A Government Jail Gang in Sydney **by Augustus Earle (1793–1838)**

transportation have been collated and indexed in P.W. Coldham's *The Complete Book of Emigrants in Bondage, 1614–1775* (GCP, 1990), but there are many others, of which those in print include J.C. Hotten's modestly titled *The Original Lists of Persons of Quality, Emigrants, Religious Exiles, Political Rebels, Serving Men Sold for a Term of Years, Apprentices, Children Stolen, Maidens Pressed and Others who went from Great Britain to the American Plantations, 1660–1700, from MSS Preserved in the State Paper Department at the PRO* (GCP, 1962). W.M. Wingfield's *The Monmouth Rebels, 1685* (Somerset Record Society, 1985) lists the men caught and sentenced to transportation (as opposed to those executed by Judge Jeffries) after the Monmouth Rebellion in 1685.

Of interest for people with Scottish ancestry are the uprisings of 1715, in favour of the exiled Prince James Stuart, and 1745, in support of his son, Bonnie Prince Charlie. Much information appears in the calendared and indexed State Papers (Domestic) and (Scotland) series at the National Archives, while records of trials of rebels are in the King's Bench records, KB 8.

Useful tip

The National Archives has 'registers of convict transportation' 1787–1867 in series HO 11, which are presently unindexed. The records will seldom state a place of origin, but often their place of conviction would not be too far from their home, so they provide reasonable clues for tracing their origins.

Case history

Joanna Lumley's Indian roots

'It seems the most normal thing in the world', wrote actress Joanna Lumley in her autobiography *Stare Back and Smile* (1989), 'to have been born in Kashmir'. Born in 1946, a year before the end of the British Raj, Joanna Lumley really wasn't unusual in coming from a British family with long links to India.

The Honourable East India Company had controlled parts of India since the 17th century, but under Robert Clive 'of India' (1725–74) it became the dominant power there. Clive retired to become MP for Shrewsbury, Shropshire, but I discovered that his career inspired many local boys, including James Rutherford Lumley, born nearby at Newport, Shropshire, in 1773, to seek their fortunes there. James became an ensign in the Honourable East India Company Service (HEICS). He fought under the future Duke of Wellington in the Second Maratha War (1803–4) that culminated in the British capture of Agra and Delhi, the seat of the old Moghul Empire. In subsequent wars of conquest in India and Java, James Lumley made a firm friend of Lt William Coventry Faithful, whose daughter Clara he later married. James and William both became Major Generals in the HEICS army: James died peacefully at Ferozepore in 1846, and William died on a sea voyage to South Africa in 1838.

The Indian Mutiny of 1857 caused many of the faint-hearted to return to Britain. James and Clara's son William Faithful Lumley became a prison chaplain in Essex, but his own son Charles returned to India as an agent for the Bank of Bengal. After the Mutiny, the HEICS was replaced by the Viceroy and India was administered, until 1947, by the Government-controlled India Office. Charles's son served as a Major in the 6th Gurkha Rifles during the Second World War, and was stationed in Kashmir in 1946, when his daughter Joanna was born.

British in India

The original records of the Honourable East India Company Service and India Office, including chaplains' returns of baptisms, marriages and burials (there was no General Registration), together with Indian directories and *India Army Lists* are all easily accessible at the India Office Library, now part of the British Library. Useful too is the *Percy Smith India Index* at the Society of Genealogists. The India Office records in fact cover British activities as far as Aden, Gulf, Burma, Afghanistan, China, Malaysia and St Helena. See M. Moir's *A General Guide to the India Office Library* (British Library, 1988) for more detail.

want to know more?

• First inhabitants: See pages 181-3 on early ancestry DNA tests and read Francis Prior's *Britain BC: Life in Britain and Ireland before the Romans* (Harper Perennial, 2003).

• Jewish ancestry: Read I. Mordy's *My Ancestors were Jewish: How Can I Find Out More About Them?* (SoG, 2nd edn, 1995) and A. Kurzweil's *From Generation to Generation: How to Trace your Jewish Genealogy and Family History* (reissued 2004 by Jossey-Bass, a Wiley imprint).

• The British abroad: Read G. Yeo's *The British Overseas: A Guide to Records of their Baptisms, Births, Marriages, Deaths and Burials Available in the United Kingdom* (Guildhall Library, 3rd edn, 1994).

• For orphans sent to Canada 1870-1949, see http://freepages.genealogy.rootsweb.com/ ~britishhomechildren.

8 Religious groups

The Church of England doubled up as a form of
state registry of baptism, marriage and burial
until 1837. Your ancestors' appearance in the
official Anglican Church records may be affected
by their religion, so knowing to which religious
groups your family has belonged can be of great
benefit in tracing family members.

Religion in Britain

Before Henry VIII's Reformation of 1534, virtually everyone in England belonged to the Catholic Church. From 1534 onwards, divisions occurred, first between the Protestant Anglicans and those who clung tenaciously to Catholicism, and from the 17th century onwards between different types of Protestant denomination.

must know

Non-Anglicans

All Christians who were not Anglicans (members of the Church of England or churches in communion with it) are generally called 'Nonconformists'. They form a significant part of most people's British ancestry.

Changing faiths

Many families changed religion as prevailing trends dictated. You may find a Catholic family becoming Anglican and then wavering back to Catholicism in the 16th century, then going from Anglican to Quaker or Presbyterian in the 17th, later having a go

King Henry VIII, instigator of the Reformation in England and Wales.

at Methodism in the 18th before returning to Anglicanism, or converting to Catholicism in the Oxford Movement of the mid-19th century, with branches later becoming Mormon, Salvation Army or plain old atheist later on. By the same token, however, each denomination had a hard core that stuck to its guns come what may, and often practised a form of religious apartheid, whereby marriages outside the same denomination were very strongly discouraged. The effect of this is that if your family tree includes one ancestor who was, say, a Quaker or Catholic, you will doubtless find yourself connected to a fascinatingly dense web of interrelated families of that denomination.

watch out!

Families appearing only occasionally in Anglican records, or not at all, may be your first indication of Nonconformist ancestry.

Which records?

Anglican parish registers actually contain a lot of Nonconformists. This is because the Church of England doubled up as a form of state registry where many baptisms, marriage and burials were performed for non-Anglicans who wanted to have the legitimacy of their offspring recorded. From 1754, all save Jews and Quakers had to marry in the Church of England. Regardless of denomination, Anglican graveyards were often the only place where you could bury people.

Thus, you will find many Nonconformist ancestors in Anglican records, but conversely you may find families appearing only spasmodically, or not at all. To learn more about them, you can use the many records that were non-denominational, from rates to poor relief and manorial records to wills.

You can also use records of the denomination itself and, where applicable, records of its persecution and penalization by the Anglican authorities. Most denominations have excellent, dedicated archives holding registers, school records, newspapers and magazines, church deeds and rolls of members. There is usually a family history society and/or a society dedicated to publishing the records (and those of the denomination's persecution). Initial enquiries through the Federation of Family History Societies and at www.cyndislist.com should get you on the right track.

Baptism certificate showing an entry extracted from the registers of the Catholic chapel at Kelvedon Hatch, Essex, and subsequently kept at St Helen's, Brentwood.

must know

Clergy records
The clergy of all denominations – who were often drawn from the most dedicated families – are usually well recorded in terms of parentage, training, work and death in published sources.

Catholics

Also called 'Papists' or 'Recusants', Catholics are generally well recorded both in their own records and in state records of their persecution. Much of both has been published by the Catholic Record Society (CRS) and is available at the Catholic Central Library.

There is a flourishing Catholic Family History Society whose address is available via the Federation of Family History Societies. Also worth a visit is the site www.catholic-genealogy.com, a portal for British Catholic ancestry.

Persecution, which started in 1559 and lasted to the mid-18th century, consisted mainly of fines for not attending Anglican services (though being a priest was technically punishable by death). Many of the relevant surviving Exchequer records are published by the CRS. A good number of Catholics are listed refusing to sign the 1641-2 Protestation Returns and the 1643 Covenant (see pages 60-3), because the former included a clause pledging loyalty to the Church of England and the latter was a declaration supporting Presbyterianism. Many Catholics joined James II in his exile at Saint-Germain-en-Laye near Paris in 1689 and appear in *Saint-Germain-en-Laye: The Parochial Registers; Jacobite Extracts 1689–1720* edited by C.E. Lart (St Catherine's, 1910) and *The Jacobite Peerage* by the Marquis de Ruvigny (1904, repr. Chales Skilton 1974).

The 1715 rebellion in favour of James II's son generated some very useful records for which printed sources are E.E. Estcourt and J.O. Payne's *The English Catholic Nonjurors of 1715* and Payne's *Records of the English Catholics of 1715* (1889) and 'Cosin's List' – *The Names of the Roman Catholic Nonjurors and Others, who Refus'd to take the Oaths to His Late Majesty King George* (J. Robinson, 1862). The 1767 national census of Catholics has been published as E.S. Worrall's *Returns of Papists 1767: Diocese of Chester* (CRS, 1980) and *Returns of Papists 1767: Dioceses of England and Wales except Chester* (CRS, 1989).

The CRS has published most of the early Catholic registers, with copies at the Catholic Central Library.

Most anti-Catholic laws were lifted by the Catholic Relief Acts of 1778 and 1791, with almost full civil rights granted by the 1829 Catholic Emancipation Act, after which many Catholic chapels were opened. By then, the number of Catholic families had dwindled to only a handful outside Lancashire and London, but much new blood came in due to the revolutions in France (from 1789 onwards) and the Irish Potato Famine of the 1840s.

Many Catholic girls became nuns; an index to these is being compiled by the Catholic Family History Society.

Protestant Nonconformists

Protestant Nonconformity arose through groups splitting off from the Church of England. The 'three denominations' of Congregationalists (also called 'Independents' or 'Separatists'), Baptists and Presbyterians trace their roots to the Elizabethan Puritans within the Church of England, who broke away completely after the failure of the Savoy Conference in 1661. Quakerism was founded by

George Fox in the 1640s. Generally, groups tended to subdivide in the 18th century and recombine in the 20th. For example:

- In the 18th century, Unitarianism broke off from the 'three denominations' and Wesleyan Methodism split away from the Anglican Church.
- In the 20th century (1972), the Congregationalists and Presbyterians combined into the United Reformed Church, whose historical library holds many records relating to what was once a proliferation of different groups.

must know

Nonconformists
A useful guide to this subject is D.J. Steel's 'Sources for Nonconformist Genealogy and Family History' in *National Index of Parish Registers* (vol. 2, Phillimore, 1973). Most Nonconformist registers date from some point after 1689. Many are deposited in National Archives series RG 4 and are included in www.familysearch.org. From 1743 to 1837 the Baptists, Presbyterians and Independents had a 'General Register of the Births of Children of Protestant Dissenters of the three Denominations' at Dr William's Library, Redcross Street, London, whose wonderfully detailed records are indexed in the Vital Records Index on www.familysearch.org.

must know

Quakers
An excellent guide is *My Ancestors were Quakers: How Can I Find Out More About Them?* by E.H. Milligan and M.J. Thomas (SoG, rev. ed., 1989).

Early persecutions are traceable through church-warden's presentments and other records in the Quarter Sessions (see p. 103) and church courts (see p. 88). The Toleration Act of 1689 guaranteed religious freedom to Protestant Nonconformists. Thousands of meeting houses, mainly of Independents, were built for the now legal 'conventicles', with licences granted by the Quarter Sessions. Baptist congregations proliferated, mainly in towns.

Quakers

The Civil War spawned many sects including Muggletonians, Ranters, Seekers, Familists, Fifth Monarchy Men and the Society of Friends, known as the Quakers. The Quakers' refusal to take oaths made them a particular subject of state hostility and many fled to Pennsylvania. Descendants of those who remained tended to join less demanding

George Fox (1624–91), founder of the Quakers, surveys London after the Great Fire in 1666.

denominations, so many modern non-Quaker families actually have some Quaker ancestry. The Quakers' wonderfully detailed records of themselves and their sufferings are best accessed via the Friends' House, London.

Moravians
Founded in Bohemia, the sect was popular in Yorkshire in the mid-18th century, with records accessible through the Moravian Church House.

Methodists
Founded by John Wesley as an evangelical preaching movement within the Anglican Church in the 1730s, Methodism split away in the 1770s and fragmented into several sub-groups, including the Countess of Huntingdon's Connection and the Bible Christians. Most were reabsorbed to form the United Methodist Church in 1857 and the Methodist Church in 1932. Ministers tended to travel around large areas in 'circuits', so their registers can encompass wide geographical areas.

must know
Methodists
A helpful guide is W. Leary's *My Ancestors were Methodist: How Can I Find Out More About Them?* (SoG, rev. edn, 1999). The Methodist Archives and Research Centre holds much useful information.

John Wesley outside Swathmore Hall by John Jewel.

Salvation Army

Founded in 1865 by William Booth, a Methodist preacher, the Salvation Army keeps its own records, including dedication of children (akin to baptisms) and commissioning of officers. These can be accessed at local Army centres and the Army's United Kingdom territorial headquarters.

The Salvation Army
by Jean Francois Raffaelli.

Mormons

The Church of Jesus Christ of Latter-day Saints was founded in New York in 1830. By 1851 there were 30,000 converts in Britain, and many more joined, although most eventually migrated to Utah. Their records, kept in branch membership books, are excellent. Mormons have a religious mission to trace all family trees so as to identify everyone who has ever lived in the context of living descendants or relatives. The latter can then hold ceremonies giving the deceased family members the opportunity of becoming Mormons, should their souls so desire.

Other denominations

Some of the many smaller sects and denominations to which your ancestors may have belonged are the Sandemanians, Cambellites, Inghamites, New Church (Swedenborgians or New Jerusalemites), Universalists, Plymouth Brethren and the Catholic Apostolic Church (or Irvingites). They and their records are described in vol. 2 of the *National Index of Parish Registers*.

want to know more?

• Walloons (Flemish Protestants) and Huguenots (French Protestants), who fled from Catholic persecution in the 16th century and sought asylum in England, are discussed on pages 133-4.
• Palatines (German Protestants) fleeing persecution arrived in England in the 17th and 18th centuries. Many went on to Ireland (see www.irishpalatines.org).
• Jewish settlers in England are discussed on pages 135-6.
• Presbyterians and their Scottish parishes are discussed on pages 60-1.

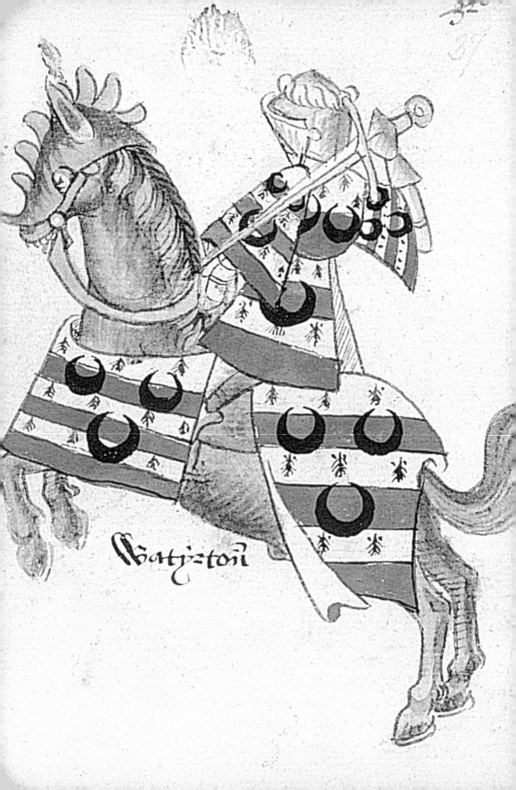

Gatijstoñ

9 Tracing even further back

Records such as wills and manorial records can take family lines back into the Middle Ages. Because of lack of surviving records, ambiguities in existing ones and widespread poverty, however, it is unusual to be able to trace the male line of a family back beyond the 16th century. If the family belonged to the upper echelons of society, however, they may be traceable a lot further back.

Royals, nobles and gentry

The records of land-holding, heraldry and blue blood provide a fascinating maze of lineages that can stretch back far into ancient times. The vast amount of well recorded family trees associated with nobility and landed gentry make the discovery of such distinguished ancestry in your own family an exciting prospect.

must know

Gateway ancestors
These were people who were non-royal, but who were themselves descended from Medieval royalty.

Following ancestral lines

As you trace back your different ancestral lines, you'll find some much harder to follow than others. Those with which you are likeliest to succeed will be the better-off families. If you trace all your family lines, you will probably find at least one that goes back – often via a series of younger sons – to a landowner, whose ancestry may then be quite easily traceable much further back. If you're lucky you'll even find intermarriages with descendants of the aristocracy, who may in turn have married 'gateway ancestors'.

Coat of arms of the House of
Hanover as Kings of Great Britain.

In fact, statistically, we must *all* be descended from Edward I, whose immediate descendants frequently married into the aristocracy, thus sending much royal blood gushing into the upper classes, which could in turn filter down through all social classes to the present. In the 13th century, the population of Britain was only about 3 million. With two parents, four grandparents, eight great-grandparents and so on, and given an average of 30 years per generation, we each have some 67 million potential ancestors from that period – about as many people as are living in Britain today. But because of the frequent intermarriage of cousins, the number of humans alive in Edward I's day from whom we're actually descended from is vastly less – probably about 3 million. Of course, logic also shows that we're all descended from the peasants at Edward I's gate too, but as their pedigrees have gone largely unrecorded, we can seldom trace back to them.

Population figures

The population of England was (roughly) 18 million in 1850, 6 million in 1750, 5.5 million in 1700, 4 million in 1600, 2 million in 1500, 4 million in 1300 and 2 million in 1200. The drop between 1500 and 1300 was due to the devastating Black Death.

Finding recorded family trees

There are many pre-recorded family histories. Besides the growing number of family websites (see pages 12–15), the Society of Genealogists' catalogue www.sog.org.uk/sogcat/index.html is a fantastic place to search (not least as it includes much unpublished material). Excellent too are the catalogues of the Mormons' Brigham Young University (www.lib.byu.edu/fhc) and the British Library (http://catalogue.bl.uk/F/?func=file &file_name=login-bl-list).

Traditional bibliographies are also worth consulting, particularly the following:

- G.W. Marshall, *The Genealogists' Guide* (repr. GPC, 1973)
- J.B. Whitmore, *A Genealogical Guide: An Index to British Pedigrees in Continuation of Marshall's Genealogists' Guide* (repr. J.B. Whitmore, 1953)
- G.B. Barrow, *The Genealogists' Guide: An Index to Printed British Pedigrees and Family Histories 1950–75* (Research Publishing Co., 1977)
- T.R. Thompson, *A Catalogue of British Family Histories* (Research Publishing Co. and SoG, 3rd edn, 1980)
- S. Raymond publishes a series of county bibliographies (S.A. & M.J. Raymond, 6 Russet Avenue, Exeter, Devon, EX1 3QB).
- M. Stuart, *Scottish Family History*, supplemented by compiler P.S. Ferguson (repr. GPC, 1978)
- *Scottish Family Histories*, National Library of Scotland (1986)
- W. Clare, *A Simple Guide to Irish Genealogy*, First compiled by the Rev. Wallace Clare, Irish Genealogical Research Society (rev. edn, R. Ffolliott, 1966).

Burke's Peerage

The backbone for recorded landed gentry and noble families are the Burke's publications – *Burke's Peerage and Baronetage*, *Burke's Landed Gentry* and associated works including *Burke's Extinct Peerage* and *Burke's Extinct Baronetage* – all available in good genealogical libraries, indexed in *Burke's Family Index* (Burke's Peerage, 1976) and increasingly available online at www.burkes-peerage.net.

The original works of John Burke, who began his publishing career in 1826, tended to give people rather fanciful ancestors, many of whom were supposed to have 'come over with the Conqueror', but actually hadn't. A century ago the fearsome scholar Horace Round (1854–1928) demolished many of these false claims and ushered in an era of much more cautious, scholarly work based rigorously in hard evidence, not hearsay – an approach you are very much urged to emulate. The more recent the Burke's publication, then, the more reliable it is likely to be.

Families with coats of arms

The (largely non-fanciful) roots of the Burke's pedigrees lay in the 'visitation pedigrees' of the king's heralds from the College of Arms. Between

Many lines of descent from royalty appear in Burke's *Royal Descents*.

The crest used, with very dubious authority, by my Hammond ancestors. Not all coats of arms and crests are genuine!

1530 and 1687, heralds travelled the country recording the family trees of those with coats of arms. Their works, now largely published by the Harleian Society and fully catalogued in C.R. Humphery-Smith's *Armigerous Ancestors and Those Who Weren't: A Catalogue of Visitation Records Together With an Index of Pedigrees, Arms and Disclaimers* (IHGS, 1997), are available in many good libraries and archives. They provide reliable family trees of knights, manorial lords and wealthy townsmen stretching back into the Middle Ages and including numerous connections back to the blue-blooded aristocracy.

Royal lineage

Many royal links – but not by any means all – were published by the Marquis of Ruvigny in his *The Blood Royal of Great Britain, Being a Roll of the Living Descendants of Edward IV and Henry VII* (T.E. Jack, 1903)

Heraldry

Many people think there are generic coats of arms for surnames, but this is not true. They in fact descend down male lines from the ancestor to whom the arms were granted, and their use is controlled strictly by the College of Arms and (in Scotland) the Court of the Lord Lyon. The best place to start looking up coats of arms for specific families is Sir B. Burke's *The General Armory of England, Scotland, Ireland and Wales* (1884). You can identify arms by breaking them down into their component parts and looking them up in *An Alphabetical Dictionary of Arms Belonging to Families of Great Britain and Ireland Forming an Extensive Ordinary of British Armorials* by J.W. Papworth and A.W. Morant (T. Richards, 1874), reprinted as *Papworth's Ordinary of British Armorials* (Tabard Publications, 1961). Excellent guides to the subject include A. Fox-Davies' *A Complete Guide to Heraldry* (J.P. Brooke-Little, 1969) and *Basic Heraldry* by S. Fryer and J. Ferguson (Bramley Books, 1993).

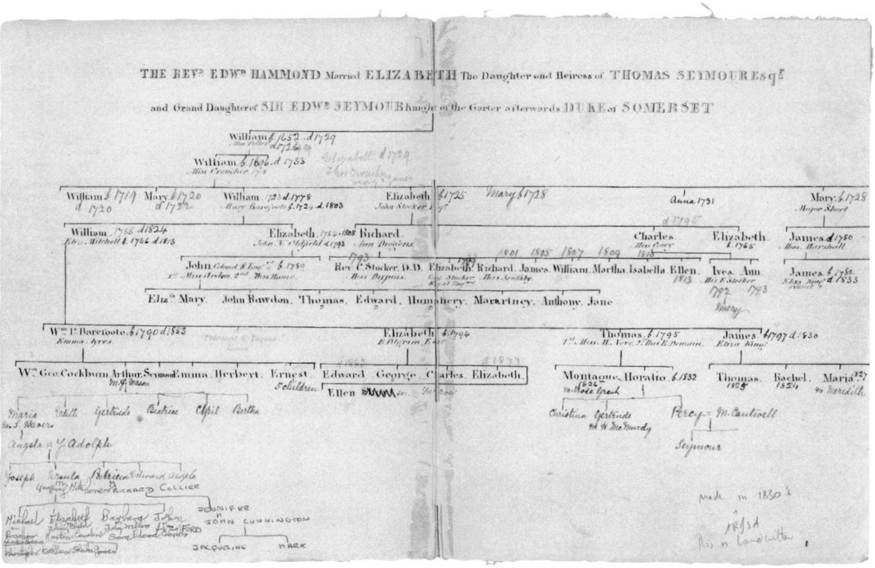
THE REVD. EDWD. HAMMOND Married ELIZABETH The Daughter and Heiress of THOMAS SEYMOUR Esqr.
and Grand Daughter of SIR EDWD. SEYMOUR Knight of the Garter afterwards DUKE of SOMERSET

Royal descents exercise such a magnetic attraction that some genealogists simply make them up. This 19th-century family pedigree, proudly updated in the 20th century, includes an entirely spurious descent from the Duke of Somerset, brother of Henry VIII's wife Jane Seymour.

Arms of my Havers ancestors, quartering those of D'Ewes and Jermyn.

and his series of volumes of *The Plantagenet Roll of the Blood Royal, Being a Complete Table of All the Descendants Now Living of Edward III, King of England*, best consulted in good libraries but also available in a rather awkward form on www.ancestry.com.

For exciting links back to royalty in Europe and beyond see Sir Iain Moncrieffe of that Ilk's fascinating *Royal Highness: Ancestry of the Royal Child* (Hamish Hamilton, 1982) and Sir Anthony Wagner's *Pedigree and Progress: Essays in the Genealogical Interpretation of History* (Phillimore, 1975). The latter shows how you can connect yourself back through the Balkans and Byzantium to the ancient Armenian princes, descended ultimately from the ancient High Kings of Parthia - the successors of the Persian Empire - in the first couple of centuries BC. The earliest certain blood ancestor who can be traced by this means is Pharnabazus I, King of Iberia (modern Georgia), who was born about 326 BC and ruled 299 to 234. We can speculate even further back, but we can't prove any earlier blood ties - though I'm working on it.

Roman lineage and beyond

Just as fascinating are the 8th and 9th century Welsh genealogies that link many modern families back to the Dark Age dynasties that arose when the Romans left these islands in 407 AD. Indeed, uncorroborated traditions incorporated in these pedigrees make links back to Romans, not least to Magnus Maximus (d. 388 AD) himself, a real historical figure who used Britain as his power-base for a successful march on Rome, where he made himself Emperor. Ultimately, lines go back via Caratacus and Cymbeline, in the

The Brutus Stone in Totnes, said to be the stone on which Brutus stepped ashore, is an eccentric commemoration of the legendary ancestor of the indigenous British.

times of the Roman invasion, and into unverifiable tradition, tracing up to Brutus, descended from Aeneas, a survivor of the fall of Troy. Brutus is said to have come ashore at Totnes, Devon, in the 2nd millennium before Christ. Even though the story probably only contains the grain of a grain of truth, it's a fantastic starting point for British genealogy.

Most Irish family traditions go back to a similar founder – Milesius. Though more of cultural interest than historical value, these traditions provide an absorbing background to all Irish genealogy and go a long way to compensate for the sad lack of so many later records there.

Pagan gods

Many ancient pedigrees trace back to gods. Julius Caesar was very proud of his own supposed descent from Aeneas, whose mother was the goddess Venus. Ancient British royalty claimed descent from the god Beli Mawr, and Saxons and Vikings from Woden. When Christianity spread, pious scholars tended to lop the pagan gods off the tops of pedigrees and replace them with descents from Noah and thus from Adam and Eve – which had the odd effect of making everyone from Jesus to Milesius appear to be reasonably close relations of each other. Bizarrely, the cutting-edge science of DNA has had a not dissimilar effect of reminding us how closely related we all actually are.

Original sources for early research

Besides already published family trees, which are helpful for links with the aristocracy in particular, you can turn to the following original sources for tracing your family back to the Middle Ages:

Taxes

Among Britain's earliest surviving records that list ordinary people are tax lists. Dating as far back as the 12th century, they take the form of poll taxes, land tax, lay subsidies, forced loans and, of course, the sheep tax of 1549. They are mostly in National Archives series E 179, catalogued at www.nationalarchives.gov.uk/e179/ with explanations of each of the records taken from

must know

Tax lists

These may provide evidence of earlier people of your surname in your ancestral village. A succession of people with the same surname in Medieval tax lists may be as close as you will get to a family tree – somewhat frustrating, as relationships won't be stated, but a good deal better than nothing.

Case history

Hugh Grant's royal ancestry

Tracing actor Hugh Grant's ancestry produced several surprises. The first was that the mild-mannered epitome of Englishness, born in Hammersmith, London, in 1960, was the son of a Scotsman, sprung from a whole line of Scottish officers in the British army, with other ancestors including Dr James Stewart (1831–1905), a missionary from Edinburgh who explored the Zambesi with Dr Livingstone.

Hugh's Englishness actually comes through his maternal grandmother, Margaret Isobel Randolph, daughter of a Kentish barrister and granddaughter of Revd. Cyril Randolph, a Kentish cricketer and rector.

Social status like that in the 19th century is often a clue that the family might appear in *Burke's Landed Gentry*, and indeed they did, under the Randolphs of Biddenden, claiming descent from an itinerant judge, Sir John Randolph, in the 14th century. Families who appear in such publications often went to great lengths to marry people of equivalent or greater status, and sure enough Revd. Cyril's wife Frances Selina was daughter of Col. Lionel Hervey, grandson of a younger son of John Hervey, 1st Earl of Bristol. By researching all the lines of the earl's ancestry, which wasn't very difficult using the pedigrees readily available in the Burke's publications, I found – after many dead ends – that the earl's wife Elizabeth Playford was a 11 x great-granddaughter of an important 'gateway ancestor', John of Gaunt, son of Edward III, thus giving Hugh Grant royal blood.

Among other well-known people with royal ancestry is singer Madonna, whose mother Madonna Louise Fortin is descended through a long line of French aristocrats from the Courtenays, a scion of the French royal family in the Middle Ages.

Lay Taxes in England and Wales 1188–1689 by
M. Jurkowski, C.L. Smith and D. Crook (PRO, 1998).
Many useful sections have been indexed at county
record offices and/or published in county record
societies: for the latter see E.L.C. Mullins' *Texts and
Calendars: An Analytical Guide to Serial Publications*
(RHS, 1958 and 1983).

Inquisitions Post Mortem

Taken from 1235 to 1649, these record the deaths of
people holding land direct from the Crown and
identify the heir, who was usually the son, making
these useful for reconstructing family trees.
Many have been published: see E.L.C. Mullins'

Church memorial to my forebear
Thomas Hawkins, Esq., Lord of
the Manor, at Boughton-under-
Blean, Kent.

Texts and Calendars... (details as before). Those for Ireland are at the Genealogical Office, Dublin (and on microfilm via Mormon Family History Centres).

Domesday Book

Compiled for William the Conqueror in 1086, this seminal English record provides details of each village and the number of freemen, slaves and others. The only people named are the tenants in chief, who held land direct from the crown, and their sub-tenants, both at the time of the Conquest (thus including many Saxon names) and in 1086, when most land had been taken by Normans. It's interesting as a background to all family trees, and the lucky few can connect their ancestry back to named individuals.

want to know more?

• You can explore the fascinating ancient British genealogies online at David Nash Ford's Early British Kingdoms website www.earlybritishkingdoms.com.
• The story of Brutus, survivor of the fall of Troy, and his descendants is recounted in Geoffrey of Monmouth's *The History of the Kings of Britain*, which is most easily available in Penguin Classics (ed. Lewis Thorpe, 1966).
• The vast corpus of genealogical material for Ireland, which was recorded before British rule put an end to the great tradition of pedigree-lore there, is preserved in works such as John O'Hart's *Irish Pedigrees* (repr. by Genealogical Publishing Company, Baltimore, 1999).

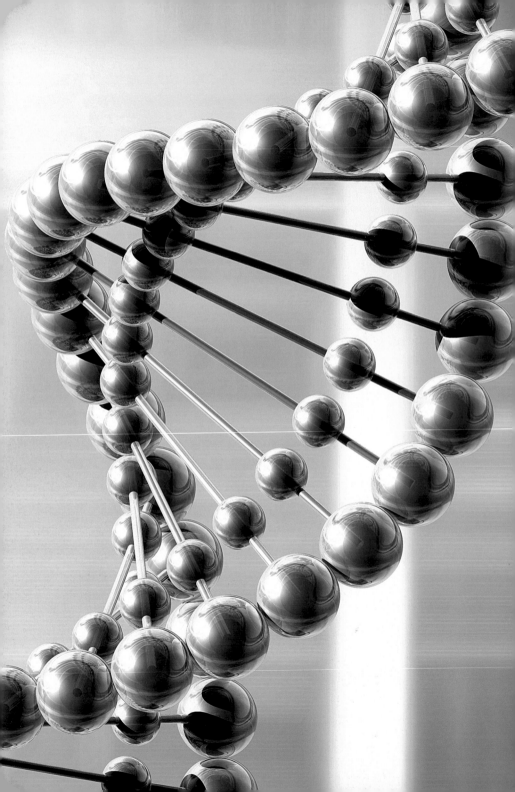

10 Surnames and DNA

Regardless of social status, names are like time capsules that we carry with us, telling us where we are from. DNA is similar. At the start of this millennium, geneticists made the new science of DNA testing commercially available to genealogists. It's an irony that the ancient subject of genealogy has been so massively invigorated by two very modern technologies, the internet and genetics. Having wondered where we came from for tens of thousands of years, it turned out that we had the secret locked in our genes all along.

What's in a name?

Forenames and surnames can tell us a lot about the ancestry and cultural origins of their bearers. Most cultures have customs governing how forenames are chosen for children, though these are now less rigidly followed in the West. A surname can suggest where a family line may have originated.

must know

Middle names
Until the mid-19th century, middle names were usual only in the middle and upper classes.

Winston Churchill, whose popularity spawned a generation of boys called Winston.

Forenames

Middle names and forenames were often passed down in families – the existence of an unusual one can help prove the link between one generation and the next. Some religious and cultural groups (such as Scottish Presbyterians) had strict naming customs that can help predict what earlier generations were called. Religious groups favoured certain sorts of name: hard-core Protestant Nonconformists favoured Old Testament names (such as Shadrach, Jeremiah and Hephzibah) and Catholics tended to opt for New Testament ones or those of more recent saints, such as Timothy, Patrick, Ambrose, Bernadette and Theresa. The less religiously-minded might choose names of famous people such as Horatio Nelson and Winston Churchill, or monarchs and their consorts: there were very few Victorias and Alberts before the mid-19th century, for example, and a vast number were so-named thereafter.

Presbyterian Scottish naming patterns

In Scotland, the eldest son was usually named after his paternal grandfather, the second son after the maternal grandfather and the third after the father. The eldest daughter was named after the maternal

Krishna Mehta with his sons Dhairendra and Shailendra. The surname Mehta is Hindu, meaning political administrator; his forename was chosen to venerate the Hindu god Krishna.

grandmother, the second daughter after the paternal grandmother and the third after the mother.

Surnames

People have had nicknames for millennia: King Arthur's father, for example, was Uther 'Pendragon', but his 'surname' did not pass down to his son. The Romans had hereditary surnames – Caesar, for example, belonged to the *gens* or family of the Julii, his given name was Gaius, and his nickname was Caesar, meaning 'hairy'. Roman custom did not outlast their rule here, and the British continued using patronymics (see page 178). Hereditary surnames only reappeared in England and the Scottish Lowlands in the 12th and 13th centuries, in the Highlands in the 18th century and Wales in the 16th century – but only becoming general there in the 19th century.

Many Medieval blacksmiths' children ended up surnamed 'Smith'.

My great-great-great-grandfather, James Paterson (d. 1887). 'Paterson' is a Scottish surname meaning 'son of Patrick'.

Surnames take five forms, all of which tell you something about your ancestry:

- Patronymics (or matronymics) are from the father's (or mother's) forenames. John, son of Roger, for example, might be surnamed Roger, Rogerson (mainly in the north) or Rogers (mainly in the south); FitzRoger if the family were Norman. In Wales, this was the most prevalent form of surname, hence ap ('son of') or verch ('daughter of') Roger.
- Occupational or 'metonymic' surnames are from occupations, such as Farmer and Fletcher (arrow maker) – many, indeed, reflect occupations now long past.
- Locative surnames point to people's places of residence or origin, such as Ashdown and Lumley, which are both place names.
- Topographical surnames were descriptions of where people lived, such as Bridge, Church and Wood, sometimes prefixed 'at' or 'atte', such as Atlee, which means 'living at the lee or clearing'.
- Sobriquets or nicknames describe people, often ironically: Black, Redhead, Wiseman and Little are all examples, but remember that Robin Hood's chum Little John was absolutely enormous!

Studying the origins of surnames often entails seeing how they were spelled in earlier times and understanding the language(s) from which they are derived. Otherwise incomprehensible surnames such as Rowed thus become clear when seen in 14th century records as 'ruh-head', showing its derivation from the Saxon for 'rough ground'.

You must at all costs lose any dogmatism about how surnames should and should not have been spelled – they were recorded in all sorts of ways and there was never a concept of what was correct or not.

Case history

Fern Britton and Philip Schofield
Surnames can change due to adoption or illegitimacy, but generally they come down male lines and can help determine where families originated. Indeed, with the help of surnames it's not uncommon to be able to work out a family's likely origins generations before the earliest proven generation on a family tree. When I traced the ancestry of presenters Philip Schofield and Fern Britton for ITV's *This Morning*, for example, I went back several hundred years, but in both cases their surnames suggested where their families originated more than 800 years ago. 'Britton' means someone who came from Brittany, quite possibly as a result of the Norman Conquest. 'Schofield' is from the Norse *skali fledr*, 'a hut in a field'. This is a popular surname east of Manchester (which is where Philip's family are from) and is indeed an area settled by Norsemen in the 10th century, hinting that Philip is likely to have at least a dose of Viking blood in his veins.

Genetics

We all inherit our appearance from our ancestors. Sometimes all you need to do is look at someone and, by studying their facial features and hair, eye or skin colour, you can make a few reasonable assumptions about where they may or may not have originated. DNA testing can be used to confirm such predictions.

must know

Chris Pomery

Chris Pomery's website www.dnaandfamilyhistory.com provides much information on DNA testing, firms, databases and what you can learn from them, as does his accompanying book *DNA and Family History: How Genetic Testing Can Advance Your Genealogical Research* (The National Archives, 2004).

How we inherit DNA

You inherit DNA from both your parents and, to varying random degrees, from your grandparents, great-grandparents and so on. The two bits of DNA that are inherited from a known source are the male or 'Y' chromosome, which men inherit from their fathers, and the mitochondrial DNA that we all inherit from our mother, regardless of our sex.

DNA testing

There are two main genealogical functions of DNA testing. The first is to check whether two people share the same genetic links. The second is to find out about our very early ancestors.

Comparative tests

These genetic tests check our direct male-to-male or female-to-female lines as follows:

(A) Test to check if you're related to someone else in the direct male line (i.e. if you each trace up your father's father's father's line, at some point you have, or suspect, a shared male ancestor).

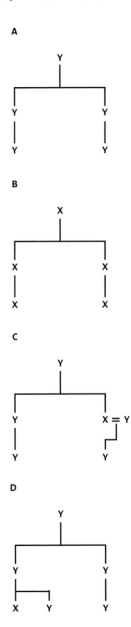

(B) Test to check if you're related to someone else in the direct female line (i.e. if you each trace up your mother's mother's mother's line, at some point you have, or suspect, a shared female ancestor).

In both cases, each person must have a DNA test. If your DNA matches, your shared ancestor is confirmed, and if it doesn't then either you don't share an ancestor, or at some point in one of the lines there has been undisclosed illegitimacy or fostering. Tests cannot be meaningfully undertaken if you don't fit these criteria. For example, there is no point having a comparative test with your father's sister's son because his father's 'Y' chromosome will have come from a different source from yours (C). Women do not inherit their father's male-line 'Y' chromosome, but they can of course have their father's, paternal uncles' or brothers' DNA tested on their behalf (D).

Early ancestry tests

These tests are on your 'deep' ancestry and can determine where your distant male and female line ancestors lived tens of thousands of years ago. You may be surprised to find that they came from the other side of the world, but more likely, if you're of British origin, you'll find that you belong to one of the core genetic populations of the British Isles, descended from the original Palaeolithic population of Europe, the Cro-Magnon 'cavemen', who came

must know

You can have your DNA tested by a wide variety of firms, such as www.familytreedna.com.

here about 10,000 years ago. Whatever your results, you'll learn how you fit into the story of the human race, which genetics, combined with studies of linguistics and archaeology, is constantly refining.

Ultimately, all genetic lineages outside Africa go back to a tiny band of people, probably numbering only a few dozen, who left Africa about (very roughly) 65,000 years ago. Together with the lineages that remained in Africa, geneticists have found that every single member of the human race goes back in the male-line to one man, dubbed the 'genetic Adam', who lived in Africa about 70,000 years ago. Equally, all female-line lineages (including that of Adam's mother) ultimately go back to the 'genetic Eve', who lived in Africa between about 100,000 and 140,000 years ago.

Both 'Adam' and 'Eve' were descended from the original, tiny core of *Homo sapiens*. Our species evolved in Africa about 200,000 years ago out of earlier *Homo* species, probably *Homo Helmei*, themselves descended from *Homo Heidelbergensis*. Other descendants of *Homo Heidelbergensis* included the Neanderthals, who lived in Ice Age Europe up to at least 28,000 years ago, and the three-foot tall *Homo floriensis*, dubbed 'Hobbits'. Their remains were found on the Southeast Asian island of Flores in 2004 and who lived until at least 18,000 years ago – and possibly a lot more recently.

Homo Heidelbergensis evolved over 2 million years ago, out of earlier *Homo* species, who were themselves descended from our *Australopithecus* forebears, about 2.5 million years ago. These diminutive, hairy ancestors of ours lived in southern and eastern Africa. They could walk upright and already made use of stones and bones as primitive

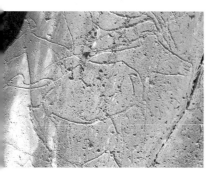

A collection of wild horses and cattle, carved on a rock in Portugal's Vale do Côa by Cro-Magnons some 22,000 years ago. The human population of Europe then was tiny, and from it came the people who later occupied Britain after the last Ice Age. This picture was very likely drawn by a direct ancestor of everyone alive now with British ancestry!

tools and weapons. They were closely akin to the ancestors of modern apes and monkeys. And so it goes back. There were single-celled organisms floating about in the primordial seas 200 million years ago who are no less ancestors of yours than your beloved granny.

But that, as they say, is another story.

want to know more?

- Surnames: For the past four years I have been compiling surname cards for *Your Family Tree*, a list of which, along with more details on surname origins, is on my website www.anthonyadolph.co.uk.
- Surname dictionaries: The best guides to surname origins are: P.H. Reaney and R.M. Wilson (eds.), *A Dictionary of English Surnames* (Oxford University Press, 2005); J. Rowlands, *Welsh Family History: A Guide to Research* (Association of Family History Societies for Wales, 2nd edn, 1997); G.F. Black, *The Surnames of Scotland: Their Origin, Meaning and History* (New York Public Library, 1946); E. MacLysaght, *The Surnames of Ireland* (Irish Academic Press, 6th edn, 1985), *Irish Families* (Irish Academic Press reprint, 1985) and *More Irish Families* (Irish Academic Press, 2nd edn).
- Our human ancestry: Much has been written on the story of our origins as revealed by DNA and recent fossil finds. Excellent accounts are: Steve Olson, *Mapping Human History – Discovering the Past through our Genes* (Bloomsbury, 2002); Spencer Wells, *The Journey of Man: A Genetic Odyssey* (Allen Lane, 2002); and Ian Tattersall, *The Fossil Trail: How We Know What We Think We Know About Human Evolution* (Oxford University Press, 1996).

Key dates in genealogy

1086 Domesday Book

1100s-1922 Manorial records

late 1100s-1600s National taxes
1662-89 Hearth Tax
1693-1963 Land Tax
1696-1851 Window Tax

1200s-1857 Wills proved in church courts
1796-1903 Inland Revenue copies of wills
1858-present Wills proved centrally

1509-present Naturalization

1534 Start of the Church of England in place of Catholicism
1538-present Parish registers in England and Wales
1653-60 Commonwealth Civil Registration
1670s Earliest Protestant Nonconformist registers
1753 Hardwicke's Marriage Act

1598-present Bishop's Transcripts

1641-2 Protestation Returns and Covenant

1660s-present Army and navy records

1697-late 1800s Settlement Certificates

1710-74 Society of Genealogists' index to apprentice indentures

1752 Calendar changed from Julian to Gregorian (1600 in Scotland): loss of 10 days and end of double dating

late 1700s-present Newspapers

late 18th-mid-20th century Directories

1823-37 Tithe Apportionments (Ireland)
1828-68 Griffith's Valuation (Ireland)

1837 (July)-present General Registration; compulsory from 1874 (England and Wales)
1845 General Registration of Irish Protestant marriages (Ireland)
1855-present General Registration (Scotland)
1864 General Registration of births, marriages and deaths (Ireland)
1868 Age at death given in General Register Office (GRO) death indexes (England and Wales)
Sept 1911 Mother's maiden name given in GRO birth indexes (England and Wales)

1839 First person photographed

1841-1901 Censuses (1911 in Ireland)

1927-present Formal Adoption records

Useful addresses

The main sources are given first followed by general sources.

Main sources
England and Wales

British Library
96 Euston Road
London NW1 2DB
tel 020 7412 7676
http://blpc.bl.uk

Church of Jesus Christ of Latter-Day Saints (Mormons)
Locations can be found on www.familysearch.org or in your local phone book. The main one is:
Hyde Park Family History Centre
64/68 Exhibition Road
South Kensington
London SW7 2PA
tel 020 7589 8561
www.familysearch.org

Family Records Centre (FRC)
1 Myddleton Street
London EC1R 1UW
tel 020 8392 5300
www.familyrecords.gov.uk/frc
(Note: The FRC is closing in 2008 and its contents are transferring to the National Archives, Kew)

Federation of Family History Societies (FFHS)
PO Box 2425
Coventry CV5 6YX
tel 024 7667 7798
www.ffhs.org.uk

Guildhall Library
Aldermanbury
London EC2P 2EJ
tel 020 7332 1868
www.cityoflondon.gov.uk

Historic Manuscripts Commission (HMC)
See National Archives
www.archon.nationalarchives.gov.uk/hmc/

Institute of Heraldic and Genealogical Studies (IHGS)
79–82 Northgate
Canterbury
Kent CT1 1BA
tel 01227 768664
www.ihgs.ac.uk

National Archives (NA)
(incorporating Historic Manuscripts Commission)
Ruskin Avenue
Kew Richmond
Surrey TW9 4DU
tel 020 8876 3444
www.nationalarchives.gov.uk

National Library of Wales (Llyfrgell Genedlaethol Cymru)
Panglais
Aberystwyth
Ceredigion SY23 3BU
tel 01970 632800
www.llgc.org.uk

Society of Genealogists (SoG)
14 Charterhouse Buildings
Goswell Road
London EC1M 7BA
tel 020 7251 8799
www.sog.org.uk

Ireland

National Archives of Ireland
Bishop Street
Dublin 8
tel 00 353 1 407 2300
www.nationalarchives.ie.

Public Record Office of Northern Ireland (PRONI)
66 Balmoral Avenue
Belfast BT9 6NY
tel 028 9025 5905
http://proni.nics.gov.uk

Scotland

National Archives of Scotland (NAS)
HM General Register House
2 Princes Street
Edinburgh EH1 3YY
tel 0131 535 1334
www.nas.gov.uk

General
England and Wales

Anglo-German Family History Society
c/o Peter Towey,
20 Skylark Rise,
Woolwell, Plymouth,
Devon PL67 5N
www.art-science.com/agfhs

Army Medals Office
Government Office Buildings,
Worcester Road, Droitwich,
Worcestershire WR9 8AU
tel 01905 772323
www.army.mod.uk

Army Museum Ogilby Trust
58 The Close, Salisbury SP1 2EX
tel 01722 332188
www.armymuseums.org.uk

Army Records Centre
Ministry of Defence, Historical Disclosure, Mail Point 400,
Kentigern House, 65 Brown Street,
Glasgow G2 8EX
tel 0141 224 3030
www.mod.uk

Barnado's After-care Department
Barnado's, Tanners Lane,
Barkingside,
Essex IG6 1QG
tel 020 8550 8822
www.barnardos.org.uk/whatwedo/aftercare

Borthwick Institute for Archives
University of York, Heslington,
York YO10 5DD
tel 01904 321166
www.york.ac.uk/inst/bihr

The British Empire and Commonwealth Museum
The Clock Tower Yard,
Temple Meads,
Bristol,
BS1 6QH,
tel 0117 925 4980
www.empiremuseum.co.uk

British Library Newspaper Library
Colindale Av., London NW9 5HE
tel 020 7412 7353
www.bl.uk/collections/newspaper
s.html

British Library, Oriental and India Office Collections
96 Euston Rd, London NW1 2DB
tel 020 7412 7873
www.bl.uk/collections/orientaland
indian.html

Business Archives Council
The Clove Building,
4 Maguire Street,
London, SE1 2NQ
tel 0207 407 6110
www.caritasdata.co.uk/charity4/
ch007084.htm

Catholic Central Library
St Michael's Abbey
Farnborough Road
Farnborough, Hants
GU14 7NQ
tel 020 7732 8379
www.catholic-library.org.uk

Catholic Family History Society
The Secretaries,
45 Gates Green Road, West
Wickham,
Bromley, Kent BR4 9DE
Catholic Record Society
c/o 12 Melbourne Place,
Wolsingham, Co. Durham
DL13 3EH
tel 01388 527747
www.catholic-history.org.uk/crs

Commonwealth War Graves Commission
2 Marlow Road, Maidenhead,
Berkshire SL6 7DX
tel 01628 634221
www.cwgc.org

Companies House
21 Bloomsbury Street, London
WC1B 3XD
tel 0870 333 3636
www.companieshouse.gov.uk

Corporation of London Record
c/o London Metropolitan Archives,
40 Northampton Road,
London EC1R 0HB
tel 020 7332 3820
wwwcityoflondon.gov.uk

Cremation Society of Great Britain
Brecon House, 16 Albion Place,
Maidstone, Kent ME14 5DZ
tel 01622 688292
www.cremation.org.uk

Dr William's Library
14 Gordon Square,
London WC1H 0AR
tel 020 7387 3727
www.dwlib.co.uk

Friends' House
173-177 Euston Road,
London NW1 2BJ
tel 020 7663 1135
www.quaker.org.uk/library

The Grand Secretary of Freemasonry
Freemasons' Hall,
Great Queen Street,
London, WC2B 5AZ
tel 0207 831 9811
www.ugle.org.uk.

Guild of One-Name Studies
c/o Society of Genealogists,
Box G, 14 Charterhouse Buildings,
Goswell Road, London EC1M 7BA
www.one-name.org

HM Land Registry
32 Lincoln's Inn Fields,
London WC2A 3PH
tel 020 7917 8888
www.landreg.gov.uk

House of Lords Record Office
Palace of Westminster,
London SW1A 0PW
tel 020 7219 3074
www.parliament.uk

Huguenot Society of Great Britain and Ireland
University College Library,
Gower Street, London WC1E 6BT
tel 020 7679 5199
www.ucl.ac.uk/library/huguenot.
htm

Imperial War Museum
Lambeth Road, London SE1 6HZ
tel 020 7416 5320
www.iwm.org.uk

India Office Library
See British Library

Law Society Library
113 Chancery Lane, London
WC2A 1PL
tel 0870 606 2511
www.library.lawsociety.org.uk

London Metropolitan Archives
40 Northampton Road,
London EC1R 0HB
tel 020 7332 3820
www.cityoflondon.gov.uk

Manorial Society of Great Britain
104 Kennington Road, London
SE11 6RE
tel 020 7735 6633
www.msgb.co.uk

Maritime History Archive
Memorial University of New
Foundland,
St John's, New Foundland A1C 5S7,
Canada
tel 00 1 709 737 8428
www.mun.ca/mha/index.php

Methodist Archives and Research Centre
John Rylands Library, University of
Manchester, Oxford Road,
Manchester M13 9PP
tel 0161 275 3764
http://www.library.manchester.ac.
uk/

Metropolitan Police Historical Museum
Unit 7 Meridian Estate, Bugsby
Way,
Charlton, London SE7 7SJ
tel 020 8305 2824
www.met.police.uk/history

Metzner, Len
3 The Thatch, Somerton,
Somerset, TA11 6SS
tel 01458 273131
metzner@enterprise.net

Moravian Church House
5 Muswell Hill, London N10 3TJ
tel 020 8883 3409
www.moravian.org

National Maritime Museum
Park Row, Greenwich,
London SE10 9NF
tel 020 8858 4422
www.nmm.ac.uk

National Portrait Gallery
St Martin's Place,
London WC2H 0HE
tel 0207 306 0055
www.npg.org.uk/search

Naval Personnel Records Office
Ministry of Defence,
CS(RM)2 Navy Search,
Bourne Avenue, Hayes,
Middlesex UB3 1RF
tel 020 8573 3831
www.mod.uk.

Office for National Statistics Library
1 Drummond Gate,
London SW1V 2QQ
www.statistics.gov.uk

Phillimore & Co. Ltd
Shopwyke Manor Barn,
Chichester, West Sussex,
PO20 2BG
tel 01243 787636
www.phillimore.co.uk

Postal Searches and Copies Department for Wills after 1858
The Probate Registry,
Castle Chambers, Clifford Street,
York YO1 9RG
tel 01904 666777

Principal Registry of the Family Division
First Avenue House,
42–49 High Holborn,
London WC1V 6NP
tel 020 7947 6980
www.courtservice.gov.uk

RAF Museum
Grahame Park Way,
Hendon, London NW9 5LL
tel 020 8205 2266
www.rafmuseum.org.uk

RAF Personnel and Training Command
Branch PG 5a(2) (for officers) and P,
Man 2b(1) (for non-officers),
RAF Innsworth,
Gloucestershire GL3 1EZ
tel 01452 712612
www.mod.uk

Robert Blatchford Publishing Ltd
33 Nursery Road,
Nether Poppleton,
York, YO26 6NN
www.genealogical.co.uk

Romany and Traveller Family History Society
c/o Mrs J Keet-Black,
6 St James Walk,
South Chailey,
East Sussex, BN8 4BU
www.rdg.ac.uk

Royal Marines Historical Records and Medals
HRORM,
Room 038, Centurion Building,
Grange Road, Gosport,
Hampshire PO13 9XA
tel 023 9270 2126
www.mod.uk

Royal Marines Museum
Eastney Barracks,
Southsea, Hampshire PO4 9PX
tel 023 9281 9385
www.royalmarinesmuseum.co.u

Royal Naval Museum
Buildings 1–7, College Road,
HM Naval Base, Portsmouth,
Hampshire PO1 3NH
tel 023 9272 7562
www.royalnavalmuseum.org

Royal Naval Personnel Records Office
Ministry of Defence,
CS(RM)2, Navy Search,
Bourne Avenue, Hayes,
Middlesex UB3 1RF
tel 020 8573 3831
www.mod.uk

Salvation Army
101 Newington Causeway,
London SE1 6BN
tel 0845 634 0101
www.salvationarmy.org.uk

United Grand Lodge of England
The Grand Secretary,
Freemasons' Hall,
60 Great Queen Street,
London WC2B 5AZ
tel 020 7831 9811
www.ugle.org.uk

United Reformed Church
Church House, 86 Tavistock Place,
London WC1H 9RT
tel 020 7916 2020
www.urc.org.uk

United Reformed Church
History Society Library
Westminster College, Madingley
Road, Cambridge CB3 0AA
tel 01223 741300
www.urc.org.uk

Ireland

Deeds Registry
Kings Inn, Henrietta Street,
Dublin 7
tel 00 353 1 804 8412
www.landregistry.ie

Federation of Services for Unmarried Parents and their Children
The Adopted Peoples Association,
27 Templeview Green,
Clare Hall, Dublin 13
tel 00 353 1 868 3020
www.adoptionireland.com

Genealogical Office
2–3 Kildare Street, Dublin 2
tel 00 353 1 603 0200
www.nli.ie

General Register Office
Joyce House, 8–11 Lombard Street
East,
Dublin 2
tel 00 353 1 635 4000
www.groireland.ie

The Grand Secretary of Freemasonry
Freemasons' Hall,
17 Molesworth Street,
Dublin 2, Eire.
tel 00 353 1 676 1337
www.irish-freemasons.org

Irish Genealogical Research Society
The Irish Club, 82 Eaton Square,
London SW1 9AJ
tel 020 7235 4164
wwww.irelandseye.com

National Library of Ireland
Kildare Street, Dublin 2
tel 00 353 1 603 0200
www.nli.ie

Registrar General of Eire
Joyce House, 8–11 Lombard Street,
Dublin 2, Eire
tel 00 353 1 635 4000
www.groireland.ie

Registrar General of Northern Ireland
Oxford House,
49–55 Chichester Street,
Belfast BT1 4HL
tel 028 9025 2000
www.groni.gov.uk

Representative Church Body Library
Braemor Park, Rathgar,
Dublin
tel 00 353 1 492 3979
www.ireland.anglican.org/library

Scotland

Birthlink
21 Castle Street, Edinburgh EH2 3DN
tel 0131 225 6441
www.birthlink.org.uk

Court of the Lord Lyon
HM New Register House,
Edinburgh EH1 3YT
tel 0131 556 7255

The Grand Secretary of Freemasonry
Freemasons' Hall,
96 George Street,
Edinburgh, EH2 4HQ
tel 0131 225 5304
www.grandlodgescotland.com

National Library of Scotland
George IV Bridge,
Edinburgh EH1 1EW
tel 0131 623 3700
www.nls.uk

Registers of Scotland Executive Agency
Erskine House, 68 Queen Street,
Edinburgh EH2 4NF
tel 0845 607 0161
www.ros.gov.uk

Registrar General of Scotland
New Register House, Charlotte Square,
Edinburgh EH1 3YT
tel 0131 334 0380
www.gro-scotland.gov.uk

Scottish Genealogical Society
15 Victoria Terrace,
Edinburgh EH1 2JL
tel 0131 220 3677
www.scotsgenealogy.com

Channel Islands

Alderney

Clerk of the Court (General Registration)
Queen Elizabeth Street,
Alderney GY9 3AA
tel 01481 822817
www.alderney.gov.gg

Guernsey

Her Majesty's Greffier (census, General Registration and wills)
General Register Office,
Royal Court House,
St Peter Port GY1 2PD
tel 01481 725277
www.gov.gg

Priaulx Library (parish registers)
Candie Road, St Peter Port GY1 1UG
tel 01481 721998
www.gov.gg/priaulx

Jersey

Jersey Library (census)
Halkett Place, St Helier JE2 4WH
tel 01534 759992
www.jsylib.gov.je

Judicial Greffe (General Registration and wills)
Royal Court House,
Royal Square,
St Helier JE1 1JG
tel 01534 502300
www.judicialgreffe.gov.je

Société Jersiaise and Lord Coutanche Library (census and parish register searches)
9 Pier Road, St Helier JE2 4UW
tel 01534 730538
www.societe-jersiaise.org

Sark

General Registrar
La Valette, Sark

Isle of Man

Chief Registrar
The General Registry,
Deemster's Walk,
Bucks Road, Douglas IM1 3AR
tel 01624 687039
www.gov.im/registeries

Manx Museum (census, parish registers and wills)
Kingswood Grove, Douglas
tel 01624 648000
www.gov.im/mnh/manxmuseum.asp

Index

Acknowledgements

The author would particularly like to thank Anna Power, Denise Bates, Dora Kneebone, Scott Crowley, Marion Fox and B.A. 'Chalky' White. The case studies are based on work originally commissioned by *Family History Monthly*, *GenesReunited* and ITV's *This Morning*.

Picture credits

The publishers would like to thank the people listed below for use of the following pictures in this book. The other pictures are from the collections of Anthony Adolph or have been sourced by the publishers. Where only a picture credit is given, identification details can be found in the caption to the illustration. BAL = Bridgeman Art Library; LMA = London Metropolitan Archive.

2 *Portrait of a Family: The Birthday of the Mother* by J. Dastine © Archivo Iconografico, S.A./CORBIS; **10** *The Edge of Sherwood Forest*, 1878 by Andrew MacCallum/Phillips, The International Fine Art Auctioneers, UK/BAL; **24** © Stuart Atkins/Rex Features; **26** *The Census at Bethlehem* by Brueghel, Musée des Beaux-Arts, Arras, France, Giraudon / BAL; **30** Census in 1949. © Hulton-Deutsch Collection/CORBIS; **32 & 33** FRC (Public Record Office); **34** © Ken McKay/Rex Features; **36** *The Wedding Breakfast* by George Elgar Hicks, Christopher Wood Gallery, London/BAL; **46** *The Westminster School of Industry, Old Pye Street*, printed by Leighton Brothers, City of Westminster Archive Centre, London/BAL; **48** © Rex Features; **50** *The Christening* by Francis Wheatley, York Museums Trust (York Art Gallery), UK/BAL; **52** *Lord Cromwell, Wearing the Order of St George* by Hans Holbein (school of)/The Trustees of the Weston Park Foundation/BAL; **57** *The Elopement* by George Morland, Christie's Images, London/BAL; **63** *Charles I in Three Positions* by Carlo Maratta after Van Dyck, The Trustees of the Weston Park Foundation/BAL; **64** NA (Public Record Office) E 179; **65** © Nils Jorgensen/Rex Features; **67** *A Dying Man Dictating his Will*, Fol.195v from *Justiniani in Fortiatum*, French School (14th century)/Biblioteca Monasterio del Escorial, Madrid, Spain, Giraudon/BAL; **73** © Bettmann/ CORBIS; **75** *Richmond Castle, Yorkshire*, by Alexander Keirincx, Yale Center for British Art, Paul Mellon Fund, USA/BAL; **76** *Month of October: Sowing*, from 'Breviarium Grimani', Fol.10v Biblioteca Marciana, Venice, Italy, photo: Roger-Viollet, Paris/BAL; **79** *The Beginning of St Luke's Gospel*, Lindisfarne Gospels, Cott Nero DIV f.139, British Library, London/BAL; **82** Archivio di Stato, Siena, Italy/Alinari/BAL; **84** © Lee Snider/CORBIS; **87** Old portrait of a family © Andy Washnik/CORBIS; **88** *House of Lords* from Ackermann's *Microcosm of London* by T. Rowlandson & A.C. Pugin/Private Collection/BAL; **92** *Mixed company patronizes a popular London coffee shop near the 'Olympic' theatre, Wych Street, Strand*, by Robert & George Cruilshank from *Life in London*, Mary Evans Picture Library; **95** LMA; **96** *Bird's-eye View of Guy's Hospital, Southwark, with Figures in the Foreground*, Guildhall Library, Corporation of London/BAL; **99** Left *The County of Norfolk*, engraved by Jodocus Hondius, Private Collection/BAL; **99** Right Detail from Camberwell and Stockwell map, reproduced from the 1913 Ordnance Survey Map; **102** *The Hanging of John Thurtell at Hertford Jail in 1824*, Anonymous/Guildhall Library, Corporation of London/BAL; **103** *Interior of the Debtor's Prison, Whitecross Street, in the 1830s*, Guildhall Art Gallery, Corporation of London/BAL; **105** Suffolk Record Office, Ipswich; **108** *The Postman* from *Costume of Great Britain*, 1805, by William Henry Pyne/Guildhall Library, Corporation of London/BAL; **110** *Fish Fags* by Thomas Rowlandson, Private Collection/BAL; **116** *The Doctor* by Arthur Miles, The Maas Gallery, London/BAL; **121** *Battle of Agincourt*, 1415 © Stapleton Collection/CORBIS; **122** © CORBIS; **123** Above *18th-century soldiers on parade outside St James's Palace* © Historical Picture Archive/CORBIS; **123** Below *Unveiling of the Royal Artillery War Memorial, London in 1925*. © Hulton-Deutsch Collection/CORBIS; **124** *Captain, Flag Officer and Commander* from *Costume of the Royal Navy and Marines*, engraved by L. and E. Mansion, Private Collection, photo: The Stapleton Collection/BAL; **126** NA (Public Record Office) ADM 188; **127** Private Collection, photo: Royal Exchange Art Gallery at Cork Street, London/BAL; **128** © Hulton-Deutsch Collection/CORBIS; **130 & 143** *In the Land of Promise* by Charles Frederic Ulrich/ Corcoran Gallery of Art, Washington DC/BAL; **134** Map of East Prussia, 1645, from *Le Theatre du Monde* or *Nouvel Atlas*, 1645, by Joan Blaeu/ Bibliotheque des Arts Decoratifs, Paris, France, photo: Archives Charmet/BAL; **135** © Mike Laye/CORBIS; **136 & 139** National Archives; **144** *A Government Jail Gang, Sydney, New South Wales, 19th century* by Augustus Earle/ Private Collection/BAL; **146** © Julian Makey/Rex Features; **150** Private Collection, photo: Philip Mould, Historical Portraits Ltd, London/BAL; **154** *Landscape in Spring, With a Nun Walking among Daffodils* by John Sowerby, Mallett & Son Antiques Ltd, London, UK/BAL; **156** © Bettmann/CORBIS; **157** *John Wesley outside Swathmore Hall* by John Jewel, Fenstone/Newport Museum and Art Gallery, South Wales/BAL; **158** *The Salvation Army* by Jean Francois Raffaelli, Private Collection, photo: Christie's Images/BAL; **160** *Jousting Knights* from *Sir Thomas Holme's book*, Harley 4205 f.37 British Library, London/BAL; **162** Private Collection, photo: The Stapleton Collection/BAL; **171** © Manou Riahnon/Rex Features; **174** © Digital Art/CORBIS; **176** © Hulton-Deutsch Collection/CORBIS; **178** Above *The Blacksmith* from *Le Livre des Echecs Moralises* by Jacques Cessoles, Ms.3066 fol.42 v Bibliotheque Municipale, Rouen, France/BAL; **179** © Michael Dunlea/Rex Features.

⟨ **Collins** need to know?

Look out for these recent titles in Collins' practical and accessible need to know? series.

Other titles in the series:

To order any of these titles, please telephone 0870 787 1732 quoting reference 263H. For further information about all Collins books, visit our website: www.collins.co.uk